ACADEMIC
LIBRARY
MANAGEMENT

ACADEMIC LIBRARY MANAGEMENT
CASE STUDIES

EDITED BY
TAMMY NICKELSON DEARIE
MICHAEL METH
ELAINE L. WESTBROOKS

Neal-Schuman

An imprint of the American Library Association

CHICAGO   2018

Extensive effort has gone into ensuring the reliability of the information in this book; however, the publisher makes no warranty, express or implied, with respect to the material contained herein.

ISBNs
978-0-8389-1559-2 (paper)
978-0-8389-1588-2 (PDF)
978-0-8389-1589-9 (ePub)
978-0-8389-1590-5 (Kindle)

Library of Congress Cataloging-in-Publication Data

Names: Dearie, Tammy Nickelson, editor. | Meth, Michael, 1978- editor. | Westbrooks, Elaine L., editor.
Title: Academic library management : case studies / edited by Tammy Nickelson Dearie, Michael Meth, Elaine L. Westbrooks.
Description: Chicago : ALA Neal-Schuman, an imprint of the American Library Association, 2018. | Includes index.
Identifiers: LCCN 2017010131 | ISBN 9780838915592 (pbk. : alk. paper)
Subjects: LCSH: Academic libraries—United States—Administration—Case studies. | Academic libraries—Administration—Case studies.
Classification: LCC Z675.U5 A35175 2017 | DDC 025.1/977—dc23 LC record available at https://lccn.loc.gov/2017010131

Text design in the Chaparral Pro, Gotham, and Bell Gothic typefaces.

♾ This paper meets the requirements of ANSI/NISO Z39.48-1992 (Permanence of Paper).

Printed in the United States of America

22 21 20 19 18   5 4 3 2 1

Contents

Acknowledgments

THE EDITORS WOULD LIKE TO EXPRESS our gratitude to Dr. Beverly Lynch, director of the Senior Fellows Program and professor in the UCLA Graduate School of Education and Information Studies, for her inspiration to create a book of case studies devoted to academic libraries.

Our thanks to the UCLA Senior Fellows Class of 2014 for support and encouragement.

We are especially thankful to our authors who graciously contributed their ideas and expertise and committed to taking on the hard work of writing the case studies, drafting revisions, and meeting numerous deadlines.

Finally, our thanks to our families, colleagues, and friends who supported us during this process. Without their generous support, this book would not have been possible.

Introduction

IN 2014, A GROUP OF FOURTEEN librarians was chosen to participate in the UCLA Senior Fellows program—one of the longest running leadership programs for academic library leaders. We brought to this three-week immersive leadership residency program a range of experiences that helped us gain insight and learn from each other. As the program progressed, we spoke to Beverly Lynch, the program director, about how our group could contribute to the profession and which opportunities she saw ahead. Her suggestion was to collect our experiences and stories in case study format so that others in academic libraries could learn how we approached and solved problems. We took her suggestion to heart, and now, a few years later, you are holding the result in your hands, whether in a physical copy or digital format.

We found this call to action of particular interest because we all have participated in a variety of leadership programs and have taught courses in iSchools in which we have noted the absence of case studies written specifically for our context as academic librarians. We hope that this book will help fill that void. In order to develop future leaders in our profession, we must provide librarians with the skills necessary to succeed in the complex world of academic libraries. The use of case studies to teach leadership skills is one method for transferring knowledge in a practical way. Case studies provide the basis for the application of ideas because such studies examine contemporary, real-life situations carefully laid out by experienced professionals.

Collected in this work are case studies that cover the broad area of academic librarianship. Topics include governance of libraries, creating new structures and spaces, managing through crisis, digital project planning, development and financial support models, how to engage the community in archives development, and the closing of branch libraries. The case studies are written in an accessible way so that you can see how the experiences of our authors apply in your own library. Case studies may also be used in a classroom setting because they are highly effective in engaging students to problem solve and to apply and test models they are being taught.

Consider keeping the following questions in mind as you read the case studies:

- What are the key issues or challenges presented?
- What is the context of the problem(s)?
- How is the context of the case study similar or dissimilar to the context of my library?
- What key facts should be considered?
- What key facts are missing?
- Who is the key decision maker?
- What alternatives are available to the decision maker?
- Which constraints is the key decision maker subject to?
- Do I agree with the resolution or solution?
- What other resolutions or solutions should I consider?
- What did I learn from the outcome?
- How can I apply what I have learned to my environment?

On behalf of the authors of the case studies, we anticipate that academic librarians, library administrators, library and information school educators, students, and facilitators or participants of professional development programs will find great value in these case studies.

We would also very much like to hear from you about how the case studies we have selected are having an impact on you or how you are using them. Furthermore, if you are interested in contributing a case study for future consideration please also contact us at casestudiesinlibrarianship@gmail.com.

We'd love to hear from you.

Tammy, Mike, and Elaine

CHARLES LYONS,
H. AUSTIN BOOTH, and
SCOTT HOLLANDER

1

Effective Shared Governance in Academic Libraries

THE UNIVERSITY AT BUFFALO (UB) is a public research university located in Western New York on the Canadian border. Founded in 1846 by Millard Fillmore as a private college, UB was incorporated into the State University of New York (SUNY) system in 1962 and has since grown to include three separate campuses and an enrollment of over twenty-nine thousand students. UB is now the largest campus in the SUNY system and serves as its flagship. A member of the Association of American Universities, UB is a research-intensive, comprehensive, doctoral-granting university that offers more than three hundred undergraduate, graduate, and professional degree programs.

The UB Libraries strive to comprise a premier academic research library that provides resources, expertise, services, and spaces that support the mission and vision of the university.

A member of the Association of Research Libraries, the UB Libraries provide access to a collection of 3.8 million print volumes, over ten thousand electronic journals, and three hundred research databases. The UB Libraries comprise a network of nine separate libraries staffed by approximately 130 personnel (both faculty and professional). The annual operating budget of the UB Libraries is nearing $20 million with an acquisitions budget close to $10 million.

In response to the changing landscape of research libraries, the UB Libraries underwent a significant reorganization in February 2015. A primary goal of the reorganization was to create an organizational structure that promotes and supports innovation, collaboration, and communication. Although the reorganization of the UB Libraries was successful in creating the foundation for a more agile and dynamic organization, it also spurred much debate about the internal processes and procedures followed when creating and implementing organizational changes. One area in particular emerged as a primary concern: shared governance. Like many institutions of higher learning, UB and the UB Libraries have long demonstrated a commitment to shared governance, an approach to decision making that strives to balance input from throughout the organization. That balance, always a delicate one, is especially tested during times of significant change or when roles of the various parties involved are not clearly defined. Because of the reorganization, issues around communication and decision making in the UB Libraries were thrown into sharp relief, causing us to reflect on how to create effective shared governance practices.

DEFINING SHARED GOVERNANCE

Defining the term *shared governance* is challenging: it is a term that means different things to different people, and there does not seem to be a generally accepted definition. Complicating matters, the concept of effective shared governance in higher education is the subject of much debate and has been evolving over time. Writing in the *Chronicle of Higher Education,* Dr. Gary Olson, then provost at Idaho State University, noted that shared governance "has come to connote two complementary and sometimes overlapping concepts: giving various groups of people a share in key decision-making processes, often through elected representation; and allowing certain groups to exercise primary responsibility for specific areas of decision making."[1]

Concepts that are related to, and often inherent in, shared governance include participatory leadership, consensus-based decision making, collegiality, and inclusiveness. These concepts are often discussed in terms of giving participants a "voice" or a "seat at the table" when important decisions about the operations and future directions of an organization are being made. In higher education, shared governance is often characterized as being under threat by several factors, including the corporatization of colleges and universities, the influence of political concerns over academic ones, and the rapid adoption of online teaching technologies.

One of the key challenges in effective shared governance has to do with balance: finding the appropriate level of involvement, influence, and input from the various parties that share in decision-making processes. Too much involvement from too many people can lead to "death by committee," slowing down the process of decision making and frustrating all involved. This excess involvement is especially important because today's academic libraries are experiencing a period of great disruption, and the ability to respond nimbly to continual change is paramount. Too much involvement can also lead to "groupthink" in which group pressures lead to forced conformity and a lack of creativity or critical thinking. On the other hand, a lack of participation can lead to more authoritarian or top-down approaches to decision making that can leave people feeling disempowered and unengaged.

SHARED GOVERNANCE IN THE UB LIBRARIES

Broadly speaking, the primary groups of people involved in shared governance and decision making in the UB Libraries can be broken down into three categories: administration, faculty, and staff (both professional and classified). The UB Libraries' administration, represented by a large Directors Council before the reorganization, is now primarily composed of five associate university librarians (AULs) and the vice provost for University Libraries (VPUL) to whom they each report. There are over forty-five faculty librarians in the UB Libraries, and they are represented by the five elected members of the Faculty Executive Committee (FEC) who serve alternating two-year terms, with two members elected in one year and three the next. There are over eighty staff members in the UB Libraries, and they are similarly represented by the five elected members of the Professional Executive Committee (PEC) who also serve alternating two-year terms. Librarians participate in university-wide governance through such structures as the Faculty Senate, the Faculty Senate Executive Committee, the Faculty Senate Library Committee, the Professional Senate, and other ad hoc and standing campus-wide committees.

Shared governance encourages involvement in decision making from all staff throughout an organization, but the focus in higher education tends to be on the relationship between faculty and administrative leadership. At many colleges and universities, it is often a fraught relationship, one that is characterized by suspicion and susceptible to mistrust. Many, though certainly not all, of the debates about shared governance issues in the UB Libraries were between administrators and faculty members (as opposed to staff members). In order to fully understand shared governance in the UB Libraries, it is important to note the significance for UB librarians of having faculty status.

In the 1960s and 1970s, SUNY librarians vigorously advocated for attaining and then retaining faculty status. During this period, movement activists described feeling like second-class citizens on their campuses and being dissatisfied because classroom faculty "saw us as technicians rather than scholarly people."[2] SUNY librarians in the faculty status battle were motivated by a variety of factors, including salary parity with professorial faculty, eligibility for tenure and sabbaticals, equivalent academic ranks to professorial faculty, voting privileges as faculty, and academic-year appointments. After much lobbying, SUNY librarians were granted academic rank, including faculty status, in 1968.

In the literature of the era, SUNY librarians stated that they hoped to obtain the "dignity and respect" associated with being considered faculty members of their academic communities. This effort included an enormous desire for more "participatory management" at the SUNY central administration level and at local campuses. SUNY librarians expressed dissatisfaction over not having meaningful input in policy making in their libraries. In essence, participation in shared governance was a major reason why SUNY librarians fought so hard for faculty status: they fully expected that after they were made faculty, decisions would be made on a more collegial and shared basis, and these expectations are still very much a part of how the UB Libraries operate today.

REORGANIZATION IN THE UB LIBRARIES

The reorganization of the UB Libraries was designed to take advantage of the opportunities created by transformations in the research library landscape in general and more specifically by changes on our own campus.

Drivers of the Reorganization

The drivers for transforming the UB Libraries' organizational structure included developing a culture that supported innovation and creating teams and workflows that encouraged collaboration and communication across previously isolated faculty and staff. In addition, we wished to create professional development opportunities for faculty and staff and develop more effective succession planning strategies in the face of anticipated retirements of key personnel. The UB Libraries also wanted to align our organizational structure with university-wide priorities identified in the university's ambitious strategic plan called "UB2020" as well as with the UB Libraries' own Balanced Scorecard strategic map.

In 2013, under the president's direction, UB2020 was moving into a new implementation phase focused on the following four areas: teaching the curriculum (specifically, a new general education curriculum), research, innovation, and infrastructure (specifically, our "Heart of the Campus" initiative that aims to create new learning landscapes throughout the campus, not just in lecture halls and laboratories). The new organizational structure of the UB Libraries was designed to reflect and respond to this four-pronged, campus-wide focus.

In addition, a survey of UB Libraries' faculty and staff and intensive follow-up focus groups, facilitated by an outside consultant, were conducted in 2013. The results of the survey, which had a very high response rate, as well as feedback from the focus groups identified five key issues we hoped to address through our reorganization:

- A clearer sense of unit missions
- More efficient decision-making structures
- Improved communication
- More collaboration across units
- Greater support for innovation

Not only did the reorganization itself promise to deliver these goals, but the job descriptions for newly created positions deliberately incorporated these goals as job responsibilities. All unit heads, for example, were charged with "creating a culture of innovation, collaboration, communication, engagement, and accountability."

In addition to surveys and focus groups, further discussion, consultation, and information sharing about the reorganization occurred throughout 2014, including library-wide Town Forums, a presentation to the university-wide Faculty Senate Library and Information Technology (IT) Committee, numerous Library Directors' Council meetings, and various e-mail communications. The VPUL also discussed the reorganization with other administrators, including the UB provost to whom she reports.

The New Organizational Structure

The reorganization of the UB Libraries was implemented in early 2015 and resulted in an organizational structure composed of five units, four of them new: Discovery and Delivery; Research, Education, and Outreach; Technology; Administration; and Law. The Law Library remained a distinct, semiautonomous unit, with the director of the Law Library continuing to report to both the VPUL and the dean of the Law School. Each new unit is headed by an AUL who reports directly to the VPUL. The AUL structure replaced a more cumbersome one composed of functional directors, functional coordinators, building-specific directors, and subject-specific directors, many of whose duties overlapped. Descriptions of the four new units follow.

The Discovery and Delivery (D&D) unit combined numerous previously isolated and organizationally separate operations: interlibrary loan, collection development, access services, technical services, and acquisitions. This unified unit focuses on delivering library materials to users at the point of need in a holistic, strategic fashion. D&D teams are arranged to more efficiently manage the workflows related to the provision of library materials: from selection and acquisition to description and discovery and, finally, to the delivery of print and online materials to our patrons.

The changing nature of academic publishing caused a rethinking of our organizational structure related to scholarly communications. The increase in open-access journals, open educational resources, and mandates to open federally funded research as well as increased interest in open data prompted the bringing together of our scholarly communication specialists with the subject liaisons who interacted with our scholars (the teaching faculty of the university) into a single unit called Research, Education, and Outreach (REO). This unit also focuses on the changing nature of the library subject liaison, especially in light of the fact that interdisciplinary research had become a priority on campus.

Instead of library IT support spread out organizationally across several different areas, the Technology unit became a single entity providing centralized technological support services for web development, digitization projects, desktop computing, and networked information delivery to all library faculty and staff. This coordinated approach eliminated duplicative services allowing library faculty and staff to focus on mission critical tasks leading to better knowledge-sharing and cooperation among departments. Finally, the Administration unit brought our human resources, finance, and facilities teams together. User demand, especially from students but also from faculty and community users, for repurposing of library space for increased high-tech collaborative study and work spaces motivated us to bring all facilities operations into a single unit so that we could fashion a master plan that prioritized and coordinated library space projects under a single vision.

GOVERNANCE CHALLENGES

As the reorganization plan took shape and especially following implementation, three key challenges emerged that caused us to reflect on the nature of truly effective shared governance. First, at a very basic level, we found ourselves reviewing and clarifying the very processes and procedures (including approvals and reviews) that needed to be followed when reorganizing in order to comply with both the bylaws and spirit of shared governance. We also engaged in deep discussions about how decisions are made regarding recruitment for the new roles created by the reorganization and about hiring in general. Finally, because effective shared governance depends on participation in decision making, we focused on ways we could create the sort of inclusive culture that encourages and facilitates broader and more meaningful participation from people throughout the organization.

Who Approves a Reorganization?

Within the larger UB organizational structure, the status of the UB Libraries as an academic unit or an administrative one is complicated by the fact that although many of our librarians have faculty status, we are not a unit that awards degrees or produces credit hours. Throughout our history, the UB Libraries have reported to the academic leadership of the university (i.e., the provost, as is currently the case) and to administrative leadership (for example, for many years we reported to the chief information officer). Within SUNY there is little consistency regarding where the library falls in the organization charts of the other sixty-three colleges and universities in the system. These facts lead to confusion about whether the UB Libraries are a support unit more akin to the Computing Center or the Teaching and Learning Center, for example, or an academic one more similar to the School of Management or the College of Arts and Sciences.

It was in this context that basic questions began to emerge concerning the proper processes and procedures that should be followed when creating and implementing a reorganization: what the process was and, in fact, whether a process even existed. These questions came to the fore during a question-and-answer session with the provost at a university-wide Faculty Senate Executive Committee (FSEC) meeting in October 2015. In particular, the provost was asked to provide clarity about the status of the UB Libraries as an academic or administrative unit and whether the "bylaws and spirit of shared governance" had been followed when the UB Libraries' reorganization was adopted. In particular, one faculty member asked if the UB Libraries reorganization should have been reviewed more closely and voted on by the Faculty Senate.

After some deliberation, the provost confirmed that the UB Libraries were indeed an administrative unit, albeit a unique one. He also confirmed that the reorganization did not need to be reviewed or voted on by the Faculty Senate and that proper procedures had been followed. In an effort to communicate more clearly about what was going on with the reorganization and allay concerns, the VPUL and the chair of FEC were invited to attend a meeting of FSEC in November 2015 at which they provided an overview of the reorganization from both the faculty and the administrative perspectives. The presentations included a time line of the processes and procedures that were followed, the rationale for the new structure, and an outline of future directions for the UB Libraries.

Although the nuances of administrative and academic units may seem trivial, the debate hit on some of the same issues that were at the heart of SUNY librarians' fight for faculty status in the late 1960s and early 1970s. Some faculty took away from the provost's remarks the idea that librarians are indeed faculty, although we lack some of the same rights. An eerily similar echo occurred when one faculty member from an academic unit said at the meeting that the university was running the risk of treating faculty librarians as "second-class citizens"—the same term that was used in the 1970s.

Recruitment Policies

In March 2015, the announcement of the new AULs served as the official launch of the reorganization. The searches for the four new AULs were internal, and formal, daylong interviews (including presentations to the entire library and interviews with the search committee, the VPUL, and other key individuals) were conducted during the second half of 2014 and into the beginning of 2015. Many faculty and staff, both within and outside the library, participated in the recruitment process by serving on search committees (there were different committees for each search), attending the presentations, and giving feedback. The Technology and Administration AUL searches were campus-wide, given that there were likely qualified candidates from units outside the UB Libraries, and the D&D and REO AUL searches were limited to the UB Libraries, given that those positions required more library-specific knowledge and skills. The head of the Law Library retained her position, and her title was changed to AUL and vice dean for Legal Information Services.

Soon after the reorganization was launched, questions began to surface about recruitment policies, in particular regarding how decisions are made about whether to perform internal or external searches for open positions. A number of issues were factored in to the decision to conduct internal searches. A significant number of faculty and staff in the UB Libraries' workforce, as in many workplaces today, are nearing retirement age or are already eligible for retirement. Leading up to the reorganization, there had been a great deal of focus on improving our succession planning with an eye toward providing faculty and staff with opportunities for advancement and rewarding career paths without having to leave UB. The thinking was that internal hiring of the AULs (and future hiring, when feasible) could positively impact morale as people would see that administrators are willing to recognize and reward employees for hard work.

Other reasons led us to have an interest in internal hiring when feasible as well. From an organizational perspective, promoting from within can be an effective way to manage and retain talent. Internal hires are also "known quantities"—they are already familiar with institutional norms and culture, and the organization is already familiar with internal candidates' personalities and skills. As a result, the hiring and on-boarding process can be smoother and quicker for internal hires than for external hires. Finally, external searches, especially national searches, are expensive and time-intensive, so for very practical reasons, internal hiring sometimes makes the most sense. This factor becomes especially compelling when national searches are performed even though there are very strong internal candidates that are highly qualified for open positions.

Although the reasoning for internal hiring was well thought out, we found out after the AULs were announced that internal searches come with risks of their own. The primary challenge we encountered with internal hiring was the potential for it to be viewed as the administration "playing favorites." When all the candidates are internal, there will be people who apply for a job but do not get it, and that outcome can create challenging scenarios that can negatively impact morale and cause disillusionment among staff. Even more to the point, when there are multiple similarly qualified applicants, there is more likelihood that some people will disagree with the selection of the job recipient, and this can lead to people questioning the validity of the search process itself. Other feedback we received noted that although our internal candidates were certainly qualified for their new jobs, there may have been better qualified candidates at other schools, and, therefore, national searches should have been conducted. Similarly, some people expressed the idea that it was more important to recruit external candidates because they were free of institutional baggage and could bring fresh perspectives and new dynamics to the UB Libraries.

Moving forward, the UB Libraries will be discussing the complicated factors that must be incorporated into decisions around hiring. Because every hiring situation is unique, it is unlikely that we will ever have a formal blanket policy dictating the manner in which we recruit staff for all openings. However, we are optimistic that by openly discussing and raising awareness of the issues that are considered when making recruitment decisions, there will be more understanding and support. As one example of this, the UB Libraries have started having listening sessions to provide all faculty and staff the opportunity to express their interests and priorities regarding searches we conduct.

Participation in Governance

The sort of participatory decision making upon which effective shared governance depends requires broad participation throughout the organization. Academic libraries are complex organizations and are more reliant than ever on a diversity of ideas, opinions, and input. Another challenge we encountered in the UB Libraries as the reorganization took shape was that we seemed to lack the sort of broad participation in governance that could draw out the perspectives and input from a wide range of staff at all levels of the organization.

Membership in certain governance committees, for example, tends to be characterized by a rotation of a small group of people relative to the overall size of our organization.

The reasons for low participation rates in the UB Libraries governance vary across the organization. Some people simply are not interested in participating and prefer to focus on what may be referred to as their "real jobs." Junior faculty members and less experienced professional staff sometimes view participation in governance bodies and committees as coming with a certain amount of risk, especially when controversial decisions need to be made or hotly debated topics arise. These staff may feel that it is safer for their careers to avoid these situations altogether.

We encountered other reasons why faculty and professional staff choose not to participate in governance bodies and committees. There is a certain amount of "committee fatigue" among some staff as well as a general feeling that shared governance, with its heavy reliance on committee work, is an inefficient way to make decisions and that this process can drag things out unnecessarily. Others feel that the committee work is wasted when their recommendations are not acted on. It can be quite dispiriting, for example, to committee members when they put in a lot of effort and work to accomplish the goals set out in a committee charge, only to see nothing come of it—their recommendations, for whatever reason, are not implemented.

Furthermore, administrative duties in general can be viewed with some level of scorn, and this, too, leads some people to stay away from governance. In the literature and in the press, the relationship between administrators and staff members (both faculty and professional) in higher education is often characterized as being somewhat tempestuous and prone to mistrust. To faculty and staff, administrators may seem too concerned about the bottom line and less interested in the broader academic missions of their institutions. To administrators, faculty and staff may seem too unconcerned about emerging budgetary restrictions and the pressing needs to rethink our missions and change the way we go about doing our business. These dynamics are certainly currently present in the UB Libraries, and the evidence indicates it's nothing especially new. However, the reorganization seems to have heightened these tensions and perhaps brought about a period of even greater reluctance for participation in governance.

One final issue worth noting has to do with professional staff in particular not having a voice. Faculty and administration tended to dominate our debates about the reorganization and shared governance, and professional staff tended not to be as vocal. Faculty involvement is crucial for the identification and implementation of innovative changes to how we operate, but professional staff members are equally important, especially in today's rapidly evolving library environment, where a blurring of the lines between faculty and nonfaculty roles is occurring. What may have once been clear, or at least clearer, demarcations between what defines a faculty role and a nonfaculty one is now becoming blurry, especially as nonfaculty personnel take on more responsibility and play increasingly important roles in decision making.

The bottom line is that shared governance without broad engagement and participation of all staff is not effective shared governance at all. Encouraging and finding appropriate ways to make sure more faculty and more professional staff members feel comfortable, engaged, and motivated to participate in governance is one of the key lessons learned. One way that FEC is addressing this issue is by reminding everyone that all meetings are open to all library faculty members and to others upon request. FEC has also started to proactively invite small groups of faculty members to attend meetings in order to provide them an opportunity to get a better understanding of how FEC works and to give feedback. Finally, "brown bag" lunch sessions will be scheduled with FEC to provide an open forum for input. Thinking bigger picture, effective shared governance should include collaboration with an even broader audience, including faculty and staff from outside the libraries, students, and the local community. The UB Libraries are undertaking a strategic planning initiative that will strive to encourage this sort of collaboration (discussed in more detail later in this case).

LOOKING TO THE FUTURE

In order to move forward, we decided to focus on three core objectives: clarifying the roles played by the various groups that participate in shared governance; intensifying our focus on ways we can communicate openly and share information broadly; and engaging in a comprehensive strategic planning process that will enable us to define, communicate, and pursue a shared vision for the future of the UB Libraries.

Understanding Roles

A crucial aspect of effective shared governance is that everyone involved needs to clearly understand their roles, and in the months after the reorganization was implemented, questions about roles in decision making began to emerge. In the UB Libraries, we seemed to lack clarity about the expectations of the parties involved in governance. In the 2015 Library Faculty Concerns Survey, for example, one-third of respondents expressed some level of confusion when asked to indicate their level of agreement with the following statement: "I understand the role of the University Libraries' Faculty Executive Committee (FEC)." Some of the confusion was due simply to a lack of awareness by staff about the activities of FEC, and this lack of awareness was likely exacerbated by the low participation rates.

This issue was explored by creating a grid that indicated the levels of responsibility that various governance structures in the UB Libraries have on different issues: sole discretion, primary responsibility, advisory, consultative, review, input, approval. Although the exercise was useful, it soon became clear that the way forward for the UB Libraries was not to divvy up duties and assign authority levels because those approaches essentially produce divided, not shared, governance. Rather, we wanted to encourage fuller collaboration and more transparent sharing of input on issues that are important to the future of the UB Libraries.

Broadly speaking, FEC's responsibilities can be distilled to two separate but equally important categories: as a watchdog of sorts, ensuring that concerns from faculty are voiced and are addressed by administration, and as a sounding board for ideas, serving an advisory function. The official charge is this:

> The Faculty Executive Committee (FEC) represents the University Libraries faculty and acts in an advisory capacity to the Vice Provost for University Libraries on all matters of interest to the University Libraries faculty, including goals and policies of the University Libraries. All Libraries' faculty members are invited to convey issues and concerns to any member of FEC.

There is value in having a place where faculty can turn when issues and concerns arise, but the group came to agree that it would be beneficial going forward to focus more on making appropriate use of FEC as an advisory group. We also agreed to communicate more broadly and clearly about the importance of FEC in effective shared governance and to support faculty education (listening sessions, brown bags, etc.) about the roles FEC plays in the operations of the UB Libraries.

Communication Is Key

Open communication is certainly a key to shared governance, but the reorganization brought to light the difficulties and complexities of communicating effectively. A fairly accurate barometer of how collaboratively an organization is functioning is the manner and frequency with which people communicate with one another, and the months after the reorganization have demonstrated a steady progression of often small yet significant changes in communication. For example, quarterly informal coffee hours were set up with the VPUL, AULs, FEC, and PEC to hear concerns and issues as well as to gather advice about strategic issues and share plans. The meetings were intended to be informal and conversational. However, when meeting minutes started to be recorded and agendas were set for future coffee hours, there was concern that the intended casual and open spirit of the coffee hours was being negatively impacted. As another example, union representatives were invited to attend a semiannual libraries faculty meeting in December 2015, which put people on guard and impacted the free flow of information.

Before the reorganization, there were issues related to the uneven flow of information, and many people felt that the amount of information they received about organizational happenings depended largely on which department or unit they were in. This situation led to some staff and departments feeling left "out of the loop" and "siloed." In an effort to improve these perceptions and to help staff keep up on the reorganization, all AULs committed to sending out regular weekly e-mail updates to their units. The other AULs were included on these e-mails, and they would in turn forward the e-mails to their own units. The updates were intended to be personalized and tailored to specific units, which was the reason that the AULs first sent them only to their own units, but staff wondered why the updates weren't simply sent out library-wide, and some felt that it was another example of siloed communication. Although this issue was easily rectified—each AUL began sharing updates more broadly through existing library-wide electronic discussion lists to ensure that all staff received the same information—it serves as an illustrative example of the communication tensions the UB Libraries were experiencing in the months after the reorganization was implemented.

As communications became increasingly strained, it became clear that a neutral, third-party mediator was worth trying in order to help get things back on track. In May 2016, the current and incoming members of FEC, the AULs, the head of human resources, and the VPUL were invited to attend sessions with a professional mediator from outside UB. The mediator spent the day in various group and individual meetings. The meetings were effective in getting the various groups of people together and encouraging open, honest dialogue. The consensus was that many important issues were discussed in a positive manner and that the sessions were helpful. As a result of the meeting, the group came up with a set of suggestions for things that needed to be done differently in order to move our working relationships in a more positive direction.

Most of the steps we collaboratively identified and agreed upon had to do with ways we could improve communication. We agreed, for example, to have more participation by PEC and FEC members in meetings with administration and vice versa. We also felt that it was important to change the method of communication, whenever possible, from e-mail to more personal formats, such as telephone and face-to-face. The listening sessions we held relating to recruitment were positively received, and we agreed to schedule more of them for other topics and at all levels of the organization. Other suggestions had to do with minimizing rumors and gossip: we committed to trying to verify and confirm before repeating any information affecting working relationships and to encouraging the idea that each person should own her communication and ideas. The final suggestions had to do with empathy: when something occurs that you do not agree with, try to see issues from the other person's perspective and to respect all participants and their various points of view.

STRATEGIC PLANNING

Another key takeaway from the mediation session was that in order to work more effectively together we needed to let go of the past. We agreed that we should strive to move the organization forward by learning from the challenges we faced in implementing our reorganization—by treating the reorganization process, in fact, as a case study regarding shared governance and decision-making processes from which we could learn.

Effective shared governance, we learned, is not about eliminating conflict—it is about recognizing that conflict is a natural part of a healthy organization, especially one that is undergoing significant transformations in how it operates. Disagreements regarding priorities and how to proceed inevitably occur during almost any major undertaking, but shared governance can potentially help an organization and its people navigate those disagreements successfully and create better, wiser, and stronger outcomes in the end. Shared governance can provide the decision-making structures and support the development of a culture in which people feel comfortable with and respect the giving and receiving of feedback if decision-making authority, feedback processes, and roles in communication are made clear from the outset.

The UB Libraries are about to undertake a strategic planning process that we have specifically designed to take advantage of the shared governance structure that exists both at the university level and within the UB Libraries, as well as to apply lessons learned from our experiences with shared governance relating to our reorganization. Our strategic planning process will be led by a steering committee charged by the provost that will include the chairs of the University Faculty Senate Library Committee and the chairs of the UB Libraries Faculty Executive Committee and the Professional Executive Committee as well as additional members from libraries and the campus community. The strategic planning process has outlined specific roles and responsibilities for the steering committee as well as the VPUL and the provost in terms of decision-making authority. By engaging faculty and staff who are directly involved in shared governance groups, as well as those who are not, in considering ways that libraries can help advance the larger missions of the institution, we hope to create a willingness to embrace shared aspirations for the UB Libraries.

NOTES

1. Gary A. Olson, "Exactly What Is 'Shared Governance'?" *Chronicle of Higher Education* (July 24, 2009): A33–A35, Academic Search Complete, EBSCOhost.

2. G. DeVinney, "The 1965–1974 Faculty Status Movement as a Professionalization Effort with Social Movement Characteristics: A Case Study of the State University of New York" (1987), available from Dissertations and Theses @ SUNY Buffalo (303618563), order no. 8727687, http://search.proquest.com/docview/303618563?accountid=14169.

K. MEGAN SHEFFIELD
and M. H. ALBRO

2

LibrariesForward

Strategic Planning in an Environment of Change

TWO OF THE MOST FUNDAMENTAL TASKS that all large organizations must complete are goal setting and strategic planning. At Clemson University Libraries, significant administrative upheaval required a strategic planning process that could produce results quickly, get library employees invested in shared goals, and strike the right balance of specificity among goals, some of which were too prescriptive and others too broad. This case study will detail the process undertaken by the LibrariesForward committee to develop its own goals and processes rather than the libraries' goals document ultimately produced by the committee. Although the situation faced by Clemson Libraries was unique, the strategies and solutions used by the strategic planning committee may be useful to other library faculty and staff who face similar challenges in their own goal-setting efforts.

CONTEXT

Clemson University (CU) is a public, land-grant university in Clemson, South Carolina, established by Thomas Green Clemson in 1889. It is ranked in the top twenty-five public universities by *U.S. News and World Report* and has a Carnegie classification of R1 (highest research activity). Clemson matriculates over 16,000 undergraduate and 4,200 graduate students with a student-to-faculty ratio of 17:1. Clemson is also the land grant university for the state of South Carolina and is nationally regarded for the quality of its undergraduate education. Engineering (and other STEM fields) as well as architecture are considered standout programs at CU.

CU has one main library (Robert Muldrow Cooper Library) and three smaller branch libraries. Cooper Library is by far the largest and consists of six floors of collections, study space, and office space. The Gunnin Architecture Library contains materials relating to art, architecture, city planning, and art history. The Education Media Center supports the School of Education with curriculum and planning materials as well as technology and learning equipment. The Special Collections Library houses materials related to the history of CU and the state of South Carolina and serves as the library's archive. In addition to the main library and these three branches, we have a Library Depot located approximately twenty minutes from campus. This location houses all off-site storage, the University Records Center, a digital imaging lab, and the offices of the technical services unit. There is also a small branch library for architecture materials in Charleston, South Carolina. All these sites are known collectively as the Libraries and are treated as a single department by the university.

The Libraries employ twenty-eight faculty, sixty-two staff, and more than seventy student workers. The employees are distributed across five different units based on their job duties; each unit reports to a unit head, who reports to the dean of the Libraries. The largest units are Information and Research Services (I&RS, which consists of circulation, reference, and interlibrary loan) and Technical Services and Collection Management (TS&CM). Special Collections is a stand-alone unit, functioning out of the Special Collections Library. Library Technology maintains the software and hardware within the library and administers the institutional repository and other digital projects. The Administrative Services unit contains human resources and administration.

Within the past two to three years, CU and the Libraries have undergone an unprecedented amount of change. In 2014, the university president retired after a fifteen-year tenure; the provost retired as well. Several deans retired or took other jobs. The structure of colleges within the university was reorganized. Also in 2014, the dean and assistant dean of the Libraries left, and as a result the Libraries were governed for a year by an interim dean before a new leadership team was hired from outside the university. The new CU administration immediately began work on a new strategic plan, tentatively titled "2020Forward." Although the previous Libraries administration had overhauled the library-wide strategic plan in 2012, the plan was not well liked by employees and, with all the organizational changes, quickly became irrelevant. As a result, the employees of the Libraries felt adrift; previous goals (which had been used heavily in internal annual review documentation) no longer existed, and many people were reluctant to commit to new directions. The organization as a whole experienced a kind of "strategic planning fatigue" after so much turmoil.

The new dean of the Libraries arrived in July 2015 to an organization of employees who were unsure of their place in the new university structure and unsure of the structure of library leadership. As a result, the new dean decided to appoint a committee that would look at the new university goals (which were still being drafted at the time), review older strategic planning documents from the Libraries, and create a new set of goals for the Libraries to work toward. To complicate things further, the committee needed to get support from coworkers for its work. In fact, the "goals committee" itself had a goal: get the Libraries' employees to come together and feel invested in the strategic planning process.

CASE STUDY

The committee tasked with developing the CU Libraries goals document was formed in mid-November 2015 and was directed to have a completed document for the dean of the Libraries by February 2016. There were many reasons for this apparent rush. First, the whole university was in such a state of flux that the new dean of the Libraries needed to start somewhere, and a new strategic planning document created by faculty and staff would give her not only a road map for future directions but also a view of what the faculty and staff themselves wanted and thought were priorities. Second, our previous goals documents were quickly becoming noticeably outdated, which meant faculty and staff annual reviews were becoming more and more difficult to complete because they were largely based on the Libraries' old goals.

This period included the two holiday breaks, during which many of the committee members were scheduled to travel, thus reducing to six weeks the effective time the team was given to complete its work. This meant that in a span of six short weeks the committee needed to meet, decide on tasks and assign them to group members, review dozens of pages of strategic planning documents, speak to unit heads about their plans for their units, and synthesize this information into a draft of a totally new document of goals for the Libraries. While it created this document, the committee had to simultaneously plan a retreat for all library employees to unveil the draft of the new goals, solicit feedback, and boost morale. The committee then needed time to incorporate feedback from the retreat into a final document for the dean. It was obvious from the committee's first meeting with the dean that time would be the constraining factor for all its activities.

The committee consisted of members from each unit of the Libraries and a mix of faculty and staff for a total of six committee members, each appointed to the committee by the dean of the Libraries. For some committee members, this project was their first opportunity to work directly with each other. We were two of the committee members: Megan Sheffield, a faculty reference librarian in the Information and Research Services unit, was the chair of the committee; Maggie Albro was a staff member in the I&RS unit working in the interlibrary loan office. There was one additional faculty member from the Technical Services and Collection Management unit on the committee. The remaining three members of the committee were all staff members; they represented Special Collections, Library Technologies, and Administration and Facilities. Every unit in the library was represented, and the faculty-to-staff ratio roughly represented that found in the larger organization. Some committee members were early in their careers, while others had worked at the Libraries for decades.

Although the group was functionally advisory to the dean, the goal was always to produce a document that the entire library could stand behind. The committee met weekly to discuss plans and work on document drafts, communicating throughout the week via e-mail and Clemson Box (a cloud storage platform adopted by CU as a location for file sharing). Due to the short turnaround, the committee decided on the following time line at the first meeting:

1. Read strategic planning documents from the university, the Libraries, and units.
2. Meet with unit heads and the dean to discuss priorities.
3. Draft the goals document and plan a retreat.
4. Host a retreat to solicit feedback on goals.
5. Incorporate feedback into a final draft of the goals.

The committee also developed a more detailed time line at the first meeting that included incremental deadlines for each step just listed and divided the reading materials. Each committee member was assigned a specific topic or document and tasked with reporting back to the committee on what had been written in other strategic planning documents or previous library goals. This "divide and conquer" approach allowed the committee to cover a lot of ground in a brief time. Committee members agreed unanimously that with such a tight time line, they could not afford to waste any time at their weekly meetings, so much of the work was done in collaborative online spaces (such as Google Docs and Clemson Box) asynchronously. These online spaces allowed us to share documents and comment, which was crucial because many of the older strategic planning documents we wanted to review were getting difficult to track down. Meetings were designated specifically for hashing out tough issues, and the committee chair had the task of making sure discussions stayed on topic.

Because the university goals document was tentatively titled "2020Forward" (a nod to the previous administration's "2020 Road Map" goals document), the committee initially called itself the Libraries2020 Strategic Planning Group. However, over the course of the planning process, the university-wide document was re-titled "ClemsonForward," at which point the Libraries group adopted "LibrariesForward." As one might expect from an environment undergoing so much change, flexibility was key to our success.

The strategic planning fatigue felt by the employees of the CU Libraries in addition to the recent changes in administration created an environment in which it was critical to involve library employees in the strategic planning process. The committee felt that faculty and staff would need to be invested in the new goals for the library to achieve success in meeting them. To best find out what other members of the library felt should be included in the goals, the committee met with the unit heads and the dean of the Libraries before the writing process began. Prior to the meeting, the unit heads were provided a condensed version of the university goals statement and a list of questions and topics to think about to provide context for the discussion.

At the unit heads meeting, the committee asked each unit head to talk about things the library is doing well, things the library should be doing, and things that were worrisome, particularly in relation to the university's goals. Unit heads were also asked about what they would like to see included in the library's strategic plan. The questions were left very open-ended because the committee felt it was important to get a wide variety of feedback and not unintentionally steer the conversation. The feedback collected at this meeting was written down and was used to guide the committee's writing process.

Initially, the committee was working to develop a list of goals for the library, limited to one or two pages, in line with the direction provided by the dean of the Libraries when the committee was formed. However, once the first rough draft had been created, many committee members were uncomfortable with this approach. The committee itself was comprised of only six people, which meant that some smaller functional teams were not represented, and the committee felt it inappropriate to set specific goals at that level for people who were not "in the room." Upon further discussions with the dean of the Libraries and unit heads, it was decided that the first draft document the committee created was too prescriptive and was more of a list of action items than goals. Therefore, this original draft was discarded, but the ideas behind the list were used to create a document that was slightly more open-ended. For example, instead of creating a goal to teach a specific number of classes or offer a certain number or type of workshops, the library instruction goal was

"Support and assess a robust literacy instruction program that teaches under-graduates not just how to locate resources but how to evaluate and document them as well." This wording allowed the instruction team members the free-dom to use their expertise to create an effective program while also meeting the larger library goal.

This document was reviewed by the committee, and drafts were revised to clarify points or alter language used. The goals were divided into the areas of undergraduate learning, graduate education, and research, which cor-responded with language used in the most recent university-wide strategic planning documents. After several weeks of work, the committee decided that this document would be the one presented to library employees.

At the recommendation of the dean, the committee organized a library-wide retreat during which the proposed strategic planning document would be presented and employees would be offered a chance to provide feedback. The organization of this retreat was a challenge for the committee given not only the short time frame for completion but the need to make the event enjoyable, because most employees lacked excitement for a mandatory strate-gic planning retreat. Committee members wanted the event to be something more exciting than just another meeting with small-group discussions, and they spent a week of their very limited planning time brainstorming meeting formats.

The library itself lacked a venue large enough to hold an all-employee meeting, and an outside location would have the advantage of being "neutral" space and offer the novelty of being outside the normal work areas. However, only a handful of university locations could be booked on short notice for a group of almost one hundred people. The committee's first choice was a new building on campus within walking distance of the library—so new, in fact, that construction had just been finished the previous month and no classes had been held there yet. However, two weeks before the Libraries' retreat at this new building, technology and scheduling issues forced the event to be postponed. As a result, the dean of the Libraries granted the committee a one-month extension, allowing for a different retreat facility to be scheduled. The committee regrouped and booked a meeting and event space at the univer-sity conference center, which meant shuttle buses had to be booked to ensure that everybody was able to attend. Once the committee had the date, time, and location confirmed, they moved quickly to finalize plans for the food, the retreat agenda, and speakers.

Coincidentally, the day before the retreat the university released the new "final" draft of its strategic plan, which followed a structure unlike that of the old documents made available to the library strategic planning committee. The new university plan used the acronym REAL to divide the goals. The areas of focus were research, engagement, academic core, and living. Although the goals in the library's document could be reassigned into the new categories, the language and focus aligned more toward the previous categories (undergraduate learning, graduate education, and research). To make the document useful for the retreat, the committee noted which new category each goal would fall into and told retreat attendees that the document would be reorganized to match this new structure created by the university.

At the retreat, the dean of the Libraries, the leader of the university's strategic planning group, and the library strategic planning committee leader each spoke for no more than ten minutes about the importance of the planning process. Library employees then were served a catered lunch before their small-group discussions began. To encourage conversation about the goals document, one committee member sat at each table but was told not to provide commentary on the document unless it was to clarify any questions raised by people at the table. To help remove any boundaries or concerns about speaking in front of people they see every day, members of the same unit were discouraged from sitting at the same table, creating a fairly equal distribution of units across all tables. Feedback from the small groups was recorded by the committee member at each table. This feedback was then combined and evaluated by the committee so adjustments could be made to the goals document to reflect what library employees wished to see. The committee members stationed at each table functioned as moderators and guided discussion away from gossip and complaints toward something more useful to shape the new goals.

The library response to the retreat was generally positive. Of ninety employees, only two missed the retreat. Participants managed to work their way through the entire new goals document, and each group had a unique perspective and talking points about the new goals. Participants at one table, for example, were very concerned about security, while those at another table were concerned about how the goals would affect graduate students' library experience in particular. Employees were also encouraged to fill out an anonymous survey or to e-mail committee members with any comments they might not have been comfortable making during the table-wide discussions. The e-mailed comments in general reflected many concerns that had already been voiced, but especially in the case of those staff members who were seated at tables moderated by their supervisors, e-mailing ensured that everyone could speak directly to the committee without censoring themselves.

Following the retreat, the committee met one more time to discuss the retreat notes, and several goals were adjusted, a few were added, and a couple were deleted. For example, one of the discussion groups at the retreat noted that we could make several straightforward changes to signs and policies that would make our building more welcoming for LGBTQ individuals as well as for families. Although this adjustment was not originally included in the goals, it seemed appropriate to make revisions to include this suggestion. Other discussion groups pointed out that building security needed upgrades, a point that had been overlooked in our draft goals for Library Facilities. Some goals were clarified or adjusted; for example, one of the goals was to "create advisory groups to counsel the dean." However, some retreat participants questioned the vague nature of this goal. Who would be in these groups, and how would the dean use this counsel? This goal had arisen from discussion with the dean herself, who expressed a desire to hear from many groups such as students, staff, and others. Following the feedback, we clarified that the Libraries should "create advisory groups (such as Student Advisory Group, Staff Advisory Group, and Faculty Advisory Group) to counsel the dean." Upon revising the language for this goal, the committee created a statement to accompany the goals and provide direction in case the goals were too vague. These documents were e-mailed to all library employees for one last feedback opportunity before the goals were turned over to the dean of the Libraries. This iterative and con- sultative process of collecting feedback and incorporating it into the goals document was invaluable for making employees feel invested in the planning process. It was crucial for employees to see that they and their colleagues, rather than administrators, were deciding where the organization's priorities should be because many library employees felt that, in the past, they had been subject to organizational changes with which they disagreed.

The biggest lesson the committee took away from this experience was that flexibility is a key success factor. Especially where event planning was concerned, prioritization allowed the committee to determine which issues could be subject to compromise (location, date, time) and which were fixed (maximized involvement by Libraries employees).

CONCLUSION

Despite the vexing issues committee members faced while creating the CU LibrariesForward Plan, they were able to work past obstacles and create a stra- tegic plan that was well received by library employees and members of the campus community. For the effort to succeed, the issues of time line, buy-in, and specificity needed to be dealt with effectively.

In order to fit the strategic planning process into the six-week time line granted, the committee used a system of incremental deadlines and asynchro- nous document editing to ensure that progress was made as efficiently as pos- sible. Open communication with the dean of the Libraries and other library leaders was critical in keeping the team on task and ensuring that deadlines were met. The committee chair met with the dean of the Libraries frequently throughout the planning process. Flexibility on the part of the committee and these leaders was critical in dealing with scheduling and document formatting.

To foster employee buy-in among a group of people facing strategic planning fatigue, the process of obtaining and using employee feedback was important. In order to obtain as much feedback as possible, the retreat was designed to mix up coworker groups, giving people access to ideas and personalities that differed from those encountered in their day-to-day environments. Moderators who were intimately familiar with the proposed goals guided groups through open-ended questions to set the stage for discussion, and the concerns and views discussed were used to mold the goals to truly address employees' needs and concerns. No matter how fatigued employees were by the process, they were happy to have their input acknowledged and felt as if their voices mattered.

The committee needed to find the balance within the document that was just right. Although the initial goals document was too specific, then too broad, the final document was just right. To find the "just right" balance, the committee aimed to give goals to the unit heads, allowing each unit to work out the specifics of how each goal would be accomplished. This structure set the framework for a document that addressed areas for advancement without being simply a to-do list.

Developing a strategic plan in an environment of change with a short time line presents a vexing situation for those undertaking the process. With flexibility, communication, and focus, a strategic plan that is well liked by employees can be built from scratch in a relatively short time.

BRIAN W. KEITH and
LAURA I. SPEARS

3

One University's Approach to Academic Library Funding

Developing an Appropriations
Model for Stability

BETWEEN 2008 AND 2012, total library expenditures at the University of Florida's peer and aspirational peer institutions increased by an average of $1 million, while library expenditures at the University of Florida (UF) George A. Smathers Libraries (the Libraries) increased by less than $8,000. Although UF is aspiring to improve its institutional rankings, the Libraries' ranking is declining because of lack of funding. UF has understood for many years that the Libraries are underfunded for their mission to support the full range of teaching, learning, research, and clinical practice at UF. Although this underfunding impacts the Libraries' operating budget, it is especially problematic for the materials budget, which is dramatically below an appropriate level because the funding has historically been inadequate and because there has been no adjustment for the annual increases in the costs for essential electronic journals, databases, and other information resources since 2008. At a time when the university is aggressively investing in preeminent faculty, seeking to grow its research funding, and establishing a new online academy, the Libraries are forced, by flat or declining funding, to continue to reduce the content made available to support the university's mission and are severely challenged in meeting the demands of students and faculty for new and improved services.

In FY 2014–15, the Libraries asked for an increase of $1.94 million in the recurring materials budget to avoid further severe cuts in the content the Libraries offer to users and to restore some of the materials that had been lost in previous cuts driven by price increases. However, the Libraries received only $1.1 million in nonrecurring funds along with a commitment to begin to address the chronic underfunding for the FY 2015–16 budget. Unfortunately, this chronic problem still exists. Currently, there is no mechanism to address the inevitable increases in the cost of content with comparable increases in funding.

This chapter is a case study of academic library funding in which various aspects of budgeting for the Libraries are examined within the context of higher education funding volatility and within the landscape of select members of the Association of Research Libraries (ARL). This approach will not only richly describe the context and circumstances of the Libraries but also identify differences across peer institutions while explaining as fully as possible the variance of the UF case from those of its ARL peers. UF Libraries' funding case exhibits theoretical anomalies when judged against the general funding model of other ARL members, thus requiring an explanation of the UF funding situation that demands descriptive details of its particular environment.[1]

Although it seems reasonable that library budgets might be relative to the growth and experiences of the university community within which the library functions, this case demonstrates that in the midst of a national recovery from the 2008 recession and combined with Florida's state-driven robust funding initiatives, UF expenditures fail to explain the funding and budget challenges faced by the Libraries.

This chapter examines two perspectives on funding for components of higher education: (a) university funding as a function of the success of the stakeholder–community relationship, and (b) development of *campus use* metrics that are proposed as an index of library impact indicators of faculty and student success as well as learning outcomes.[2] Then we present our model that combines the two views, asserting that in some way, library fortunes are reliant on and related to university funding. Using a multiple regression model of library and university expenditures, along with analysis of time-series trend models, this study seeks to establish a foundation for understanding the relationship between the funding of the University of Florida and that of the Libraries and examines the campus demand statistics during the same period that includes the fiscal years 2008–9 through 2012–13.

CONTEXT

The Libraries of the University of Florida form the largest information resource system in the state of Florida. The UF Libraries consist of seven libraries; six are in the system known as the George A. Smathers Libraries at the University of Florida. Collectively, the UF Libraries (the Smathers Libraries and the Legal Information Center) hold or provide access to more than 5.45 million print volumes and 1.25 million e-books with a total library expenditure of more than $30 million while employing more than 270 full-time faculty and staff. The UF Libraries are a member of the Association of Research Libraries (ARL)—ranking number 38 on the latest ARL Library Investment Index[3]—the Center for Research Libraries (CRL), and the Association of Southeastern Research Libraries (ASERL).

The Carnegie Foundation for the Advancement of Teaching classifies the University of Florida as an R1 institution (highest research activity) with comprehensive programs in medicine and veterinary medicine as well as a "more selective" undergraduate selection process.[4] The Florida Board of Governors designated UF as a preeminent university; it is home to sixteen academic colleges and almost two hundred research centers and institutes.

As state funding for the university decreased, the budget challenges were distributed among the academic and administrative support units. Academic libraries commonly cite the insurmountable increase in electronic resources costs as the exemplar of the consequences of diminished funding for higher education. The cost of scholarly communication is enveloped by this economic challenge because research funding is increasingly reliant on open access to data and articles as a result of publishing costs falling on researchers and funders.[5] *Library Journal* confirms that although budgets have improved from 2009 recession lows, they remain well below levels required to keep up with inflation—and with increasing e-resources costs.[6]

The ability of libraries to establish a viable funding model and then advocate for it is not only diminished by limited university resources but also hampered by the political and policy-based processes of higher education funding and by historic funding models and legacies of past decisions.

The first model examines factors relating to higher education context and institutional relationships with the community of stakeholders using community engagement as one criterion in rational choice decisions made by state funders in their appropriations to universities.[7] The consequential appropriation of funds from the institution to university libraries is examined with the premise that a similar logical relationship exists and is represented as correlations between university expenditures and library expenditures.

The relationships between campus demand and use statistics are presented in a second model that asserts that library funding should be more program-driven, relying on a formula-based budget that reflects library contributions with metrics developed relating to library programs.[8] This approach would negate the invisible economic and political factors that drive most funding in higher education and directly connect the library's contributions to academic needs.

The UF Libraries sought to restore funding that had been lost beginning with the 2006–7 fiscal year budget. Since 2010, when UF adopted responsibility centered management (RCM), the Libraries have used the budgeting process as an opportunity to present a case for increased funds to redress chronic shortfalls and position the Libraries to pass that investment on to better serve user needs.

By examining a cohort of peer institutions, UF library leadership presented a variety of comparisons demonstrating that although most academic library budgets are related to university appropriation levels, the Libraries' budget began with a significant shortfall and that the relationship of library funding to university revenues was frequently volatile and inexplicable.

This study seeks to answer questions about relationships between academic library funding and the parent institution: What relationships best explain university library funding levels? In what ways, if any, can library demand statistics be useful in establishing the contribution of the academic library to the university community such that there is greater transparency in library appropriations?

Using several years of extensive state-, university-, and library-level fiscal analysis, UF library leaders have developed a strategic model that integrates peer comparisons that would facilitate the growth of the Libraries and support the university's strategic plans for improving national rankings of universities.[9]

Allen and Dickie examined state support for public colleges and universities between 1984 and 2004.[10] The authors employed twenty-three predictors that demonstrate the annual changes in state appropriations and identified the relationship between higher education institution funding and respective state support based on state economic health, state agency completion, and legislative partisanship. The study concluded with a community engagement framework to explain the higher education funding anomalies, demonstrating that state appropriations could be predicted based on a university's demonstration of community engagement.

It is clear that higher education funding operates within the same ambivalent environment as do academic libraries. But the question can be asked whether this situation is unavoidable. Are university budgets seeking to satisfy as many diverse stakeholders as does a state governing body? In fact in Florida, there is a state legislature and a board of governors. In order to promote a competitive strategy for both university- and library-level fiscal planning, in what ways does analysis of costs, benefits, and values influence decision making relating to appropriations? Weerts's study provides one way to understand the complexity of strategic planning at the university or library level, and it lays the groundwork for the use of institutional peer rankings to assess the funding shortfalls of the UF Libraries.[11]

Weerts examined growth trends in library expenditures presumed to be a result of increasing expenditures by the library's university. By showing average growth from year to year, the model seeks to predict expenditure increases by holding other variables constant. Weerts conceded that strict quantitative analysis like this assumes that increases in funding advance the efforts of the university to achieve its mission, but he argued that this type of analysis illustrates that the impact of or return on "marginal dollars allocated to the severely underfunded library" may be high—a good investment by the institution.[12]

These studies suggest that refocusing library funding advocacy from library activity measures to broader university measures makes library accountability more transparent and demonstrates the library's impact on the larger university community. UF library administration has undertaken similar measures to address the Libraries' capacity to support the university's mission and has established metrics not only for describing the state of the libraries but also, by examining regression models and campus demand statistics, for establishing a basis of comparison to peers.

CASE STUDY

The data presented represent a small but meaningful portion of the annual budget analysis efforts conducted by the UF Libraries. Used to conduct these analyses are the State University System of Florida's funding history and the ARL Annual Library Statistics Analytics data sets for the years 2008 through 2013.[13]

We examined the following:

- The state higher education funding landscape with adjusted trend charts
- A multiple linear regression using the dependent variable of total library expenditures and the university expenditures as the independent variable, across multiple cohorts (see figure 3.1)
- The correlations and coefficients for each member of one select cohort

This chapter presents a broad analysis of data sets in an attempt to provide multiple ways to view the overarching higher education landscape, the differences among a group of ranked institutions, and the volatility each library experiences with its parent university. We attempt to understand the benefits and limitations of statistical analysis of library output measures in order to create stronger funding messages and drive evidence-based decision making.

Cohorts

For the initial regression procedure, we examined three unique cohorts (table 3.1); group A then was examined more closely to demonstrate correlation and explanatory trends.

The comparative sample used three sets of Association of American Universities (AAU) public universities comprising peer groups for UF. Group A is made up of six comparable universities from the 2013 top public universities.[14] All the institutions in group A and group B were selected because they are comprehensive institutions with law schools and two or more health colleges. Other comparably ranked public institutions were excluded because they did not have these units or had atypical funding models. Group C is a list of peers provided by UF executive leadership that has been used for previous peer comparisons.

TABLE 3.1

Peer cohorts to the University of Florida

A Top U.S. Public Universities	B Top 25 Public Universities	C UF Aspirational Peer Universities
Illinois at Urbana	Michigan	California at Berkeley
Michigan	Minnesota	Illinois at Urbana
North Carolina	North Carolina	Indiana
Pennsylvania State	Ohio State	Michigan
Virginia	Pennsylvania State	North Carolina
Wisconsin	Pittsburgh	Ohio State
	Texas	Pennsylvania State
	Virginia	Texas
	Washington	Texas A&M
	Wisconsin	Virginia
		Wisconsin

State of Florida Higher Education Funding Trends

To establish an understanding of the state of Florida's higher education appropriations trends, State University System of Florida funding per UF full-time equivalent (FTE) student peaked in FY 2006–7 at $13,249; from 2007 to 2009, UF student enrollment and funding per FTE decreased 4 percent to $12,669. Allocations per FTE have begun to rise again but have experienced some inconsistency. Student enrollment at UF remains below prerecession levels, with the most recent reporting fiscal year, 2014–15, listing 45,306 FTE students. Funding sources include general appropriations, state lottery funds, student tuition, and other state trust funds. These funding sources exhibit variability, leading to increasing dependence on student tuition as a revenue source from 2007 until 2014. In 2014, despite increases in state general revenues funding, the dependence on tuition funding remained.

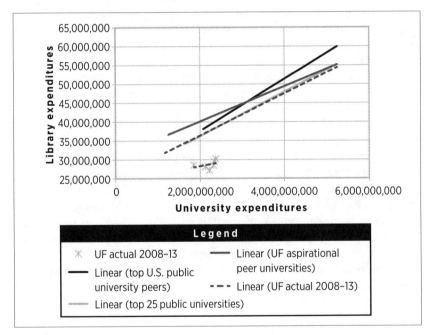

FIGURE 3.1
FY 2008/09–FY 2012/13 Peer average and University of Florida (UF) actual total library expenditures compared with total university expenditures

Peer Comparisons for University and Library Expenditures

The initial analysis conducted by the UF Libraries focused on the relationship between library expenditures and university expenditures for UF and the three peer groups. Linear regression analysis for the UF peers shows a positive and predictive relationship between university funding, as reflected in total university expenditures from all sources of funds, and library funding, as reflected in total library expenditures within the peer groups. In comparison, the UF total and UF Libraries expenditures were plotted for the five-year period 2008–2013. At UF, the library expenditures fall well below the best-fit line for all peer groups, and the positive relationship is muted. This analysis demonstrates the poor comparative standing of UF funding, as represented by expenditures, with that of its peers. It also depicts the inconsistent relationship between library expenditures and university expenditures. For group A and group B, this estimated relationship is highly significant. The relationship between library expenditures and university expenditures is moderately strong for group C. Notably, there is no significant relationship at UF between university expenditures, which have increased over time, and library expenditures. These data show that UF Libraries' funding is at levels that are much lower than those of any of the peer groups and, further, that local library funding is inconsistent with university funding.

The R-squared values reported in table 3.2 indicate the proportion of the difference in library expenditures that is predictable by differences in university expenditures. The table presents two five-year rolling averages as an indication of the type of volatility that UF Libraries experience from year to year compared with the peer groups. For group A and group B, this estimated relationship is highly significant. The relationship between library expenditures and university expenditures is moderately strong for group C. Notably, there is no significant relationship at UF between university expenditures, which have increased over time, and library expenditures.

To more closely examine each of the peer institutions, we regressed each institution's expenditures with its library expenditures, rather than just

TABLE 3.2

Coefficients of determination for rolling five-year periods

	A Top U.S. Public Universities	B Top 25 Public Universities	C UF Aspirational Peer Universities	UF Actual
2008–2012	$R^2 = 0.8675$	$R^2 = 0.6674$	$R^2 = 0.4854$	$R^2 = 0.16057$
2009–2013	$R^2 = 0.861$	$R^2 = 0.692$	$R^2 = 0.540$	$R^2 = 0.53865$

comparing with the cohort. This approach allowed us to determine whether each university library in the cohort experienced similar volatility within its own appropriations landscape. The data in table 3.3 present the actual regression trends for each of the six peer universities within group A as a further example of the inconsistency of library funding for many institutions. For the period 2008–2013, the correlation (R statistic) and the explanatory power of the independent variable (i.e., university expenditures) expressed as the R^2 statistic both show a weak relationship, and a resulting low R^2 indicates that this variable does not account for the level of library expenditures. The R statistic illustrates the strength of the relationship of the variables; R^2 suggests how much of the library expenditures can be explained by university

TABLE 3.3

Five-year regression trends

| | **2008–2012** | | | |
	Correlation Statistic (R)	**Coefficient of Determination (R²)**	**Constant**	**Sig. (p Value)**
Florida	0.0258	0.1606	26,973,984	0.0134
Illinois at Urbana	0.7119	0.8437	4,803,235	0.7506
Michigan	0.658	0.8112	10,802,695	0.7367
North Carolina	0.3107	0.5574	50,396,357	0.0097
Pennsylvania State	0.5799	0.7615	39,476,133	0.004
Virginia	0.3101	0.5568	51,231,197	0.0431
Wisconsin	0.4757	0.6897	75,400,425	0.0363
	2009–2013			
	Correlation Statistic (R)	**Coefficient of Determination (R²)**	**Constant**	**Sig. (p Value)**
Florida	0.7339	0.5387	9,293,297	0.4374
Illinois at Urbana	0.7232	0.523	21,741,507	0.1673
Michigan	0.7346	0.5396	11,199,106	0.7105
North Carolina	0.21	0.0441	45,210,807	0.0367
Pennsylvania State	0.6633	0.4399	39,206,669	0.0124
Virginia	0.0374	0.0014	33,810,329	0.0734
Wisconsin	0.7402	0.5479	92,031,903	0.0431

appropriations. UF Libraries as well as the libraries at the University of Virginia and the University of North Carolina all demonstrate inconsistent and weak performance in both of the rolling five-year analyses.

As table 3.3 also depicts, for the years 2008–2012, UF, the University of North Carolina, Pennsylvania State University, the University of Virginia, and the University of Wisconsin have results in which the linear correlation is significant; for 2009–2013, only North Carolina, Penn State, and Wisconsin demonstrate a significant linear correlation between library expenditures and university expenditures. Although the constants (intercepts) are reported and would normally be used to predict future library expenditures, these are generally meaningless, especially for multiple years of weak correlations.

The correlations illustrated in figures 3.2 through 3.5 indicate the proportion of the difference in library expenditures that is predictable by differences in university expenditures, presenting two five-year rolling averages as an indication of the type of volatility that UF Libraries experience from year to year as compared to the peer groups.

For the years 2008–2012, UF, North Carolina, Penn State, Virginia, and Wisconsin have results in which the linear correlation is significant; for 2009–2013, only North Carolina, Penn State, and Wisconsin demonstrate a significant linear correlation between library expenditures and university expenditures. Figures 3.3 and 3.4 visually depict the strength of the relationships represented by the R statistic for the five-year periods of 2008–2012 and 2009–2013, respectively. These years were chosen because UF library administration sought to demonstrate both the volatility of the relationships and the extreme inequity of overall funding between the UF Libraries and their peers.

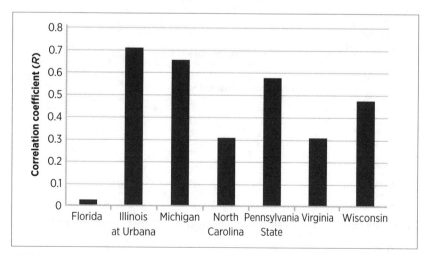

FIGURE 3.2

Five-year regression results trend, 2008–2012, R coefficients

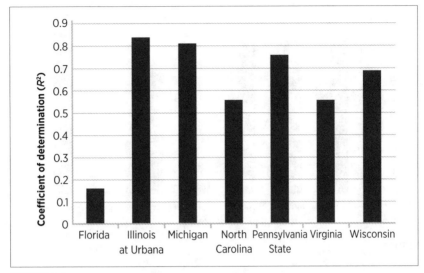

FIGURE 3.3

Five-year regression results trend, 2008–2012, R^2 coefficients

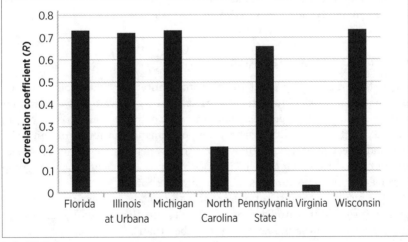

FIGURE 3.4

Five-year regression results trend, 2009–2013, R coefficients

In figure 3.3, the relationship between the UF Libraries and the university can be readily perceived as weak. This relationship as shown in the figure 3.4 years of 2009–2013 strengthens dramatically. Notably, North Carolina and Virginia are depicted with moderate relationships in 2008–2012, but those relationships weaken dramatically in 2009–2013.

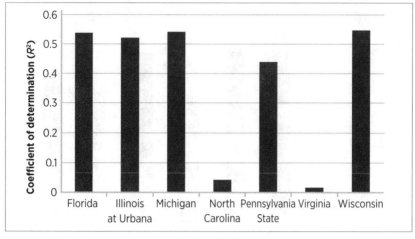

FIGURE 3.5

Five-year regression results trend, 2009–2013, R^2 coefficients

Although the results are not statistically significant in each case, the results demonstrate the unpredictability of library expenditures and the resulting inability of libraries to explain the rationale for expenditures.

Campus Demand Statistics

The data in table 3.4 present the National Center for Education Statistics' designated university characteristics that serve as indicators of demand for library resources and services, while the ARL data for library resources, in table 3.5, reflect the ability to satisfy campus demand. In the case of university demand, every indicator for UF is above the average for the six group A peer institutions.[15] However, the UF Libraries' resources are below the peer group averages for every resource, as the percentages show.

For faculty, peer institutions are able to provide, on average, 4.9 monographs for each one provided by UF; faculty are also served by an average of two fewer librarians per faculty member than at the peer institutions, with only one librarian for every 2.9 peer institution librarians available for research and instruction support. Students in peer institutions have, on average, almost five times as many monographs (1:4.9) and two-and-a-half times more librarian support. All categories of stakeholders are dramatically underserved by information technology because the range of hardware and software expenditures is anywhere from 3.8 to one for faculty to a high of fourteen to one for doctoral students. The ratios depict that in almost every category, students are served by dramatically fewer resources at UF compared with group A peer institutions.

TABLE 3.4

University of Florida demand and resources compared with peers

University of Florida demand compared with peers (%)						
	2008	2009	2010	2011	2012	2013
Total faculty	132	129	129	131	131	132
Total students	138	135	132	130	131	130
Undergraduates	131	126	121	120	120	120
Graduate students	156	155	157	156	158	155
Doctorates awarded	188	179	191	185	165	165

University of Florida library resources compared with peers (%)						
	2008	2009	2010	2011	2012	2013
Volumes held	56	53	53	52	53	52
Librarians and professional staff	61	57	59	54	54	54
Paraprofessional staff	78	74	82	78	81	78
Total staff	71	67	72	68	69	68
Materials expenditures	80	76	76	84	77	74
Total library expenditures	66	64	61	65	64	68

TABLE 3.5

Library resources: University of Florida (UF) compared with peer institutions

	PER FACULTY			PER STUDENT		
	UF	Average	Ratio	UF	Average	Ratio
Volumes held	880	2,557	1:29	98	243	01:02.5
Monographs acquired	4.28	21.02	1:4.9	0.47	2.34	1:2.3
Librarians and professional staff	0.017	0.0497	01:02.9	0.0019	0.0046	01:02.4
Other staff	0.0307	0.0545	01:01.8	0.0034	0.0057	01:01.7
Total staff	0.0477	0.1042	01:02.2	0.0053	0.0103	1:02
Materials expenditures	$2,361	$4,376	01:01.9	$262	$446	01:01.7
Total library expenditures	$5,454	$11,957	01:02.2	$606	$1,198	1:02

CONCLUSION

The findings of this study graphically demonstrate the relationship of university funding decisions to the appropriations outcomes of the libraries, for UF's peers as well as for UF. Further, the university's strategic planning documents emphasize the intent of the university to improve its overall rankings in acknowledged national rankings systems; therefore, the comparison with peer universities is a valid means to understand the Libraries' competitive footing and ability to contribute to the university's mission. These descriptions were used in multiple presentations to UF leadership as a means to demonstrate the context of the UF Libraries' challenges.

Explaining Funding Levels

What relationships best explain university library funding levels? Depending on the stakeholder in question, the framework that best explains university library funding levels at UF may be comprised of both the Weerts holistic approach and the comparison of campus demand statistics with peers. For the university leadership, the emphasis on national rankings and comparisons with some semblance of a peer cohort is very well served by statistical analysis of the relationship between university expenditures and library expenditures. Because national rankings have become a greater focus of the university's strategic plan and because the state of Florida has recovered from the recession of the past decade, the Florida Board of Governors has designated funds to the university to bolster research and innovation efforts. The strategies chosen by university leadership are to invest a majority of these funds in attracting high-profile faculty with extensive research expertise and to build competencies in innovation practices that leverage research discoveries and successes into commercial products or services that benefit a large, practical portion of Florida's communities.

If comparison with peer institutions is seen as an effective dashboard for the guiding of all university efforts, then comparison with those institutions' libraries, for expenditures and for resulting library resources, is a reasonable way to understand the mechanisms that assist and impede the Libraries' efforts to support the university's mission. Although the assessment and evaluation processes and programs that demonstrate academic library value are relatively new for the UF Libraries and for peer institutions, a research stream is beginning that supports the connection between a strong library presence and positive impacts on student learning outcomes, achievements, and successes.

Using Demand Statistics

In what ways, if any, can library demand statistics be useful in establishing the contribution of the academic library to the university community to create greater transparency in library appropriations? As the campus demand findings indicate, the university serves 55 percent more graduate students and an average of 72 percent more doctoral students than its peers. For a university with a claim to preeminence in funding and support for innovation and research, this level of research support is not competitive with that of UF's peer institutions. Although the boost of faculty expertise is important, the lack of information technology (IT) and materials support may be an area of concern, especially for students with scholarly and financial commitments to graduate programs. The attraction to a preeminent research institution would have to be weighed against the funding of the UF Libraries, which stands at less than 70 percent of the average for institutional peers. The value of the library resources percentage comparisons and the ratios provide targeted areas for further analysis and action. As the Libraries continue to build capacity for assessment, innovative data management, scholarly communications, and digital collection building, on top of an already forward-thinking use of space (i.e., shared storage facilities) and the exemplary and robust discovery services (e.g., building a linked data infrastructure), the Libraries can analyze and address competencies that support the university's mission to be as highly ranked as possible.

Next Steps for the UF Libraries

Based on the findings of this research and feedback from university leadership, we are focusing on the types of library services that are expected and the library offerings that may be most desired. For instance, before moving our overnight library hours between two campus branches, we surveyed students and faculty for their preferences. As indicated by the findings in this study, traditional resources lack support—is this an oversight, or does the library need to pivot to other, more desirable offerings? A needs assessment of faculty and graduate students, especially focused on their use of space, may direct the actions of library administration.

If the RCM budget model remains the mechanism for UF, the Libraries could question the disparity between the research resources subsidized by each of the colleges and the costs of their related library resources because then accountability by college would be simple to derive. We can examine whether the disparity between university expenditures and library expenditures is related to the perceived value of the library to the university's mission.

The Libraries will benefit from more extensive self-assessment, outreach, and communication of core values and services that directly support the mission of the university. Research can begin with an assessment of faculty and graduate student needs for library services and resources, all the while mindful that highly intensive research institutions are less successful at conveying their usefulness to their stakeholders. But as the most recent funding years suggest, the state legislature and the supervisory Florida Board of Governors have increased appropriations to the university, yet these funds have not made their way into increased library funding.

Nevertheless, the Libraries have aggressively pursued new roles for librarians, establishing positions for a data management librarian, a metadata librarian, an assessment librarian, and an informatics librarian, among others. These new specialty, hybrid librarian positions are designed to reinvent the programs and establish new initiatives in data curation, developing new collaborations and relationships that extend the Libraries' capacity to support the university's interdisciplinary research and technology initiatives.

Further comparative analysis of peers might take advantage of the research and assessment development occurring in such esteemed academic locations as Duke University, which boasts a fully articulated assessment department with acknowledged best practices for user experience research; in addition, The Ohio State University and the University of Minnesota consistently present at assessment conferences and in industry webinars on their development of organizational dashboards and strong campus collaborations, establishing connections between library services and resources and student learning outcomes.

NOTES

1. As many academic libraries seek out and test innovative ways to establish and communicate library impact, the models of Weerts and of Allen and Dickie are both nuanced approaches using a theoretical framework (in the former) and inferential statistics based on library surrogates (in the latter). The methods used by the UF Libraries assume a hybrid approach, attempting to demonstrate usefulness to the community through campus demand statistics yet using inferential analysis to demonstrate that inconsistent and opaque funding does not support the level of resources supplied by the peer institutions that the university seeks to perform alongside. With the numerous pressures and competing priorities for university funding, it is hard to determine whether these budget illustrations influence funding. But it is clear that library leaders believe that a path to greater transparency and assessment will better serve library decision making. Library initiatives, such as the establishment of specialty librarian positions, extend this foundational statistical and campus demand analysis to demonstrate library support and creation of innovative campus outreach. Combined with strong, experienced library liaison and instruction programs and comprehensive and diverse collections, the Libraries' efforts to

capture and analyze library value will, it is hoped, impact future library resources positively. See State University System of Florida, "Legislative Budget Requests and Appropriations," www.flbog.edu/board/office/budget/appropriations_budget .php.

2. David J. Weerts, "State Funding and the Engaged University: Understanding Community Engagement and State Appropriations for Higher Education," *Review of Higher Education* 38 (2014): 133–69; Frank R. Allen and Mark Dickie, "Toward a Formula-Based Model for Academic Library Funding: Statistical Significance and Implications of a Model Based upon Institutional Characteristics," *College and Research Libraries* 68 (2007): 170–82.

3. Association of Research Libraries, *ARL Statistics: Annual Library Statistics,* https:// www.arlstatistics.org/dashboard.

4. The Carnegie Classification of Institutions of Higher Education, http:// carnegieclassifications.iu.edu/.

5. Stephen Bosch and Kittie Henderson, "Whole Lotta Shakin' Goin' On: Periodicals Price Survey 2015," *Library Journal* (April 23, 2015), http://lj.libraryjournal.com/ 2015/04/publishing/whole-lotta-shakin-goin-on-periodicals-price-survey -2015/#_.

6. Ibid.

7. Weerts, "State Funding."

8. Allen and Dickie, "Toward a Formula-Based Model."

9. George A. Smathers Libraries, *Strategic Directions* (October 2014), cms.uflib.ufl .edu/portals/communications/Strategic-directions-complete.pdf.

10. Allen and Dickie, "Toward a Formula-Based Model."

11. Weerts, "State Funding."

12. Ibid.

13. Association of Research Libraries, *ARL Statistics: Annual Library Statistics,* https://www.arlstatistics.org/home; Florida State University, "Summary of State Education and General Operating Appropriations and Actual FTE Students," www.flbog.edu/board/office/budget/docs/Funding-per-FTE-SUS-and-Univ_1985 -2016.xlsx.

14. Robert Morse, "Which Universities Are Ranked Highest by College Officials?" *U.S. News & World Report,* https://www.usnews.com/education/blogs/college -rankings-blog/2013/02/28/which-universities-are-ranked-highest-by -college-officials.

15. National Center for Education Statistics, "Library Statistics Program," https:// nces.ed.gov/surveys/libraries/academic.asp.

YOLANDA L. COOPER and
CATHERINE L. MURRAY-RUST

4

A Shared Collection and the Advancement of a Collaborative Future

IN MARCH 2016 TWO INSTITUTIONS of higher education dedicated a new joint Library Service Facility (LSF). The completion of the facility provides an example in the development of a public-private partnership. The joint facility was not the two institutions' first effort to collaborate—they have a long-standing partnership in several areas, including a joint degree program. All efforts at collaboration have had a significant impact on how both institutions work together and complement each other. The development of a strong collaboration relies on building a shared vision and goals and is rife with both success and challenge. This case study demonstrates how, through compromise and dedication, both institutions completed the first phase of what will evolve into a more extensive collaboration for both university libraries and outlines the activities, processes, and operations implemented during the development to complete the collaboration successfully.

CAMPUS AND LIBRARY PROFILES

Institution A is a private university, established in 1836, with three main campuses in the state. It currently has nine academic divisions, including the College of Arts and Sciences; several professional schools; and one of the largest health-care systems in the state. The university has a Carnegie classification of R1 (highest research activity) and is cited for high scientific performance. In 1995, it joined the Association of American Universities (AAU). Currently the university has 13,000 academic staff, 7,800 undergraduate students, and 6,900 graduate and professional students . A member of the Association of Research Libraries (www.arl.org), the library has ten campus locations with holdings that include more than 4.2 million volumes, 80,000 electronic journals, and 700,000 electronic books and employs 275 professional and support staff. The main library also houses an internationally renowned special collection. With a strong liberal arts program, long-form scholarship and special collections are of great importance and necessary for student and faculty engagement. Faculty at institution A believe collections should be preserved for future generations. The majority of holdings can be found in the main library as well as the health sciences library. At the start of discussions regarding the project, both libraries were full to capacity. Two off-site storage locations had been established to contain and preserve overflow holdings that were "low and no use" materials. One of the storage facilities can be described as a basic warehouse environment. Although close to the main library, the space was inadequate for growth and had an increasingly faulty heating, ventilation, and air conditioning system. This facility held general collections from the majority of the libraries on campus as well as special collections. Materials were also housed in leased space in a nearby museum. Although this space provided a much better environment for preservation, it was farther away from campus and costly—with a tentative lease. In the proposed project, institution A would initially focus on relocating the materials located in the two storage areas to the new facility. The new facility would provide optimal preservation space to include an integrated, climate-controlled system with temperatures in the archival module at an average of 50 degrees with 30 percent relative humidity, air circulation and filtering devices, UV-shielded fluorescent lamps, and acid-neutral book storage trays. Although a good number of materials would be housed at the new facility, the majority of print materials for institution A would continue to be housed in the campus libraries.

Institution B is a public research university, founded in 1885. Like institution A, it is rated R1 in the Carnegie classification and is a member of the AAU. It has six colleges, including engineering, design, and liberal arts. Current enrollment is fifteen thousand undergraduates and eleven thousand graduate students. Institution B is also a member of the Association of Research Libraries. The library collection is now more than 97 percent electronic. Institution

B planned to relocate approximately 95 percent of the collection in paper and microform along with archival materials to the LSF. In 2011 after more than twelve years of planning and construction, the undergraduate learning commons, which is connected on two floors to institution B's main library, opened its doors. The library was given responsibility for managing the building in partnership with several academic service units. The building houses forty-one classrooms and laboratories as well as several services focused on first- and second-year undergraduates. In 2012 the library produced a study entitled *Library 2020*. Because the report concluded that more than 97 percent of the current collections are electronic only and the paper collections are seldom used, the library leadership proposed to move a significant percentage of the collections off-site to allow for the renovation of the buildings and the creation of more space for people and services. With these goals in mind, the library is currently embarking on a library renewal project at 100 percent construction that was formally initiated in 2016. The anticipated date for completion and reopening of the renovated library is January 2021. New services are being developed and piloted along with a complete reorganization of staff and library faculty. The collaboration with institution A was positioned as the opportunity to house the collections in a high-quality preservation environment while freeing space for the radical transformation of the library buildings on campus and a transformation of library services for research and learning.

PROBLEM AND PROMISE

In 2008 after the financial crisis experienced by many libraries across the United States, both institutions were in the midst of recovery and in need of a new planning strategy to accommodate limited budgets for library processes and operations. It was at this time that conversations were initiated concerning how to collaborate across institutions to leverage resources and improve services and collections while streamlining operations. The two library leaders convened working groups that were focused on a number of operational areas. Each focus group was comprised of library and managerial staff from both institutions who were focused on common interests. By 2012 after much discussion, storage and collections emerged as the most pressing issues. With that in mind analysis of the collections was completed with surprising results—there was only a 17 percent overlap in collections across both institutions. Because of such a small percentage of overlap, collections sharing became an excellent area on which to focus. Outcomes would be mutually beneficial for both institutions, and, in the long term, both could take advantage of the expertise available that allowed for expanding the service capacity for both campuses. The advantages would be substantial and allow both campus communities new opportunities to increase resources in emerging disciplines and previously underserved areas.

Following a change in leadership in the library and in the provost position at institution A, the dean of libraries at institution B met with the interim head of the libraries at institution A to continue the collaboration and focus on the proposal for constructing a high-density storage facility. Both agreed to advocate for this proposal with their campus leadership. With a solid relationship between the two university presidents already established and a record of previous collaboration in other areas, broad support followed, and the project began to move quickly. It was determined that going forward the collaboration could build on the fact that a tax-exempt, nonprofit 501(c)(3) organization had been previously established for research purposes, thus creating a structure to share financial responsibility. In 2001 AB Inc. (not the real name) had been established to facilitate joint programs between the two institutions. It was suggested that the same entity could provide structure for future collaboration across the libraries, beginning with the development of the shared collection. Once AB Inc. was reconstituted, both institutions gained equal control in the stand-alone entity through the governance and approval of a board. The president of each institution appointed three directors to the board, and both institutions bore equally the corporate and legal costs of the reorganization.

In the months that followed, both institutions participated in a feasibility study for a shared storage facility. Several potential building sites were identified, and rental real estate was considered. Throughout the process, staff from a variety of organizations on both campuses, including legal, real estate, capital planning, architectural services, and the libraries, worked closely together to move the project through the activities and layers of approvals required at both institutions. To further structure the collaboration, both institutions agreed on the following goals for the project:

- Provide a state-of-the-art, long-term facility for housing appropriate library collections.
- Expand the materials offerings to each institution.
- Reduce redundancy by establishing jointly owned collections whenever possible and as permitted by state law.
- Free up valuable central campus space.
- Improve faculty and student access and service through the appropriate use of technology.
- Do so in a manner that is strategic and economically efficient.

With the direction set it was now time for the two institutions to fully implement the project working together across all areas from administration to facilities. Moving forward, the project would require good organization, communication, and strong relationships; both institutions would establish a long-term commitment and cultural exchange.

SOLUTIONS FOR PROGRAM IMPLEMENTATION

To house materials for long-term preservation and to leverage resources, a new high-density storage facility was needed by both institutions. The facility would provide an optimum environment for storage and allow for the reutilization of space on both campuses to address the changing needs of users and to enhance access and services. High-level objectives were defined as follows:

> **One location:** Both institutions will operate a shared off-site collection at a single location.
>
> **One collection:** All items at the LSF will be merged into and managed as a single collection for the benefit of the faculty and students at both institutions.
>
> **Optimal storage:** Storage conditions at the LSF will be optimal for the cost-effective, long-term retention and preservation of multiple formats.
>
> **Robust services:** LSF services will provide users with timely access to requested materials.
>
> **Future growth:** The LSF will accommodate all future growth of physical collections.

To advise on the project, we sought consultants with deep experience. Fortunately, we soon identified two highly qualified individuals willing to take part in the project. They were then hired from another university to assist in all aspects of the planning, most especially in estimating the effort the libraries would need to handle the collections and to prepare the staff for the transition. Several project components took place simultaneously, including architect and construction management selection, site visits, project management, legal and financial planning, and library preparations. The project would require architects and construction management firms with experience in similar facilities built for other major research universities.

STRATEGY AND STRUCTURE

One of the first steps in moving forward with the joint facility was to develop a Step One proposal to submit to campus leadership for approval. The Step One proposal is the first deliverable in the capital project process. The following goals were addressed in the proposal:

- Develop a statement of facility requirements, including an opening day minimum build-out as well as a long-term final expansion.
- Study several proposed sites on each campus to determine the best location for the proposed facility.
- Build and jointly operate a high-density warehouse facility for paper and microfilm retrospective collections.
- Manage a shared collection in a shared facility. Consolidate collections, reduce overlap and duplication, enhance document delivery services, and create shared discovery tools and services to ensure ease of access and use by faculty, students, and scholars.
- Release library space on the central campus for faculty and students and for manuscripts, archives, and rare books.

The feasibility study was implemented to determine the overall program requirements for the off-site facility, including collection space, staff space, user space, building envelope, and environmental conditions. The study defined the initial opening-day build-out as well as a final program expansion, construction and expansion opportunities at three different sites, delivery and access issues to and from the site, and site conditions that would potentially impact site use for long-term storage of retrospective physical collections. The study also determined facility and system requirements for certification at the Leadership in Energy and Environmental Design (LEED) Silver level. After many options were considered, the study, begun in the fall of 2012, resulted in the selection of a site in the southwest corner of institution A's nearby property, approximately one mile from the main campus. It is approximately 4.6 miles between the two institutions.

Both institutions worked in tandem on the selection of an architect and the development of requirements. In July 2013 institution A solicited consultant qualification packages for the construction of a new LSF. The request invited consultants to submit qualifications for the broad scope of work. After all packages were reviewed, the architects were chosen. Due to the site location, institution A acted on behalf of both institutions as the developer of the facility responsible for implementing the project from conception to completion. AB Inc. financed the site lease and construction. After construction is complete, AB Inc. will lease the completed facility back to the institutions individually. To outline the collaborative arrangements, a services agreement was created that will be renewed annually to outline the LSF and collections, management duties, all costs and expenses, employment, insurance, budget, termination, and renewals.

PLANNING AND PROJECT MANAGEMENT

A project of this magnitude requires a great deal of planning and facilitation; therefore, we engaged the project management office (PMO) from institution A. The PMO provides skilled program and project managers to facilitate the entire project management life cycle. The PMO assigned a program manager and two project managers to focus on two other major areas of the project—construction and technology. Once assigned to the project, the program manager developed a charter and scope statement for the overarching program and each of the associated projects based on the Step One proposal, the request for qualifications, and other information derived from the project planning. Institution B also assigned a program manager from the library to manage the outcomes of the established working groups. Each group was convened to represent each relevant area for both institutions. The following groups were created:

> The Collection Preparation Working Group determined cataloging as well as marking and barcoding specifications along with preservation specifications. In addition, the group determined standards for physical processing, established requirements of load-in for the new facility, validated that standards were followed, and managed exceptions.

> The Logistics and Planograph Working Group prepared data for the planography to map the existing collection into the LSC. The group built estimate requirements for future growth and developed plans for the move.

> The Operations and Management Working Group developed standards for ingest and flow of materials. It also developed budgets, staffing requirements, resource plans for the new organization unit, and a plan for management of the facility.

> The Communication/Public Relations Working Group developed a plan for communicating with the institutions' user communities and the larger community during planning, construction, and initial operations.

> The Service Planning Working Group developed a service model for fulfillment and service policies.

> The Shared Collections: Retrospective Working Group developed a policy on duplication and sequencing for ingest to hand off to cataloging along with collection development policies for shared collections. It also decided what to retain, developed a process for weeding and collections management, developed a special policy for gifts, and worked to refresh current policies.

The Shared Collections: Prospective Working Group developed collection development policies for shared collections, including physical collections and electronic resources. It will work to uncover opportunities for joint licensing, determine how to deal with demand-driven acquisitions, and audit current resources.

The Systems and Inventory Control Working Group worked with the inventory system and Ex Libris Alma, the library management system, to ensure interoperability, identify interoperable pieces, and determine protocol for systems support.

The Facilities Planning, Design, and Construction Working Group coordinated and participated in the programming, design, construction, occupancy, warranty, and closing of the LSF.

All working groups were composed of representatives from both institutions who met weekly or more often based on the work at hand. It was determined later that some of these groups would continue after the project and become standing subcommittees to assist in future investigation and decisions for operations and services. In addition to the working groups, other groups were convened to assist with project coordination and communication internally for each institution and as a combined effort. The AB Inc. board met periodically to approve the major milestones of the project, including the approval of the financial strategies, design, memorandum of understanding (MOU), and construction.

The LSF steering committee became the overarching decision-making group for the program. It met monthly to review progress and decide on construction, operations, and design during the entire life cycle of the project. The committee was composed of library leadership from both institutions and the leads for each of the working groups. The project managers for construction of the facility and for technology as well as the chair of the AB Inc. board also attended these meetings as needed. Because most meetings took place through videoconference, the program manager worked before each meeting to provide the appropriate information and initiate necessary discussions to expedite the process and decision making at the steering committee meetings. Documentation was shared and edited and policies drafted and made available through institution A's cloud technology Box (www.box.com/home). The in-person meetings took place quarterly.

Each institution also met internally to coordinate activities. The coordination group at institution A met weekly to exchange information, work through processes and priorities, and talk through problems. This meeting was attended by the university librarian, the program manager, and each of the institution B co-chairs for all working groups. The coordination meeting was convened by the program manager and was also attended by the project manager for technology. Later in the project, the manager for ingest and operations for the LSF as well as the LSF operations manager also attended the meeting.

It was particularly helpful that the program and project managers facilitated the majority of the working group and steering committee meetings. This action ensured coordination and objectivity in decision making and in the review of all progress and issues.

SHARED COLLECTION

In planning for the shared collection, many questions emerged about sustainability, process, and guidelines to ensure consistency. Based on these discussions, it was determined that establishing the shared collection would require the creation of agreed-upon policies and governance to maintain the collection and outline parameters. Both institutions charged the working groups focused on collections to map out the specifics of an agreement in an MOU. This document defined the shared print collection, library participants, time line for the MOU, governance, deposit guidelines, discovery, holdings disclosure, and the guidelines for withdrawal and deselection of materials. In the MOU, the shared collection initially included physical materials housed at the LSF. Eventually, as resource sharing is expanded through online access, the shared collection will include all materials from institution A's main library and health sciences library as well as all print from institution B. Due to the challenges regarding circulation, the special collections and media collections from both institutions were excluded from the shared collection. It was also understood that not all collections in the shared print collection would be available to all patron types.

DESIGN AND CONSTRUCTION

The LSF's design had to be flexible to accommodate collection growth and to adapt to the services taking place there. Services include ingest and retrieval, scanning and delivery, and a reading room that is available for research and review. The design of the archive module was based on the Harvard model (see the Harvard Depository at http://hul.harvard.edu/hd/pages/facility .html) focusing mainly on storage and preservation and including all technical requirements—maximum foreseeable loss walls, sprinklers, and size. The LSF architects expanded on this model, noting that although the archive module is important, processing the materials and providing services are equally important. With that in mind the architects focused the "AB Inc. model" on integrating the processing center with the archive module. The processing center focuses on how materials are received, handled, and moved in and out of the archive module and considers how staff access the facility as well as the use of trucks that are picking up and delivering materials.

Taking all requirements into consideration, the LSF was designed with the following specifications: the facility is a 55,000-square-foot, secure, and climate-controlled building with state-of-the-art equipment and technology to house special and general library collections. The archive module covers 30,000 square feet and is capable of holding up to four million volumes. Initially this space would accommodate 95 percent of the collections from institution B as well as its collections in storage. Within the facility, 25,000 square feet were designated for processing materials and for special handling of those materials. Special areas include a blast freezer to stabilize any materials damaged by water and to prevent potential insect infestations; film storage to provide cold temperature conditions to lengthen the lifespan of rare films; and an intake room to isolate new materials to address any problem items before accessioning to the archive module. With the LSF housing a significant portion of materials from both institutions, it was imperative for both campuses to have in-person access to the materials on and off campus. With that requirement in mind, a reading room was added to allow users to consult materials on-site. Because the facility is off campus, staff spaces that include a wellness room and a lounge were also added.

FACILITY OPERATIONS PLANNING

With the building under construction, working groups began planning the specifics of the staffing and technology necessary to operate the facility. Because materials would be housed from both institutions, we determined that it would be necessary to have staff from both institutions working in the facility. In staffing discussions, a number of concerns were noted, including the possibility that an individual might be supervised by someone from the other institution who is following a different set of policies designed to support a public institution and vice versa. It became increasingly clear that having employees from both institutions would be challenging. It would also be challenging to determine how librarians would work at the facility given that librarians at institution B have faculty status while librarians at institution A are staff but faculty-equivalent. Although requirements for rank are similar at both institutions, there are differences in their respective processes and approvals. There are also differences in benefits. To simplify the staffing, it was suggested that institution B oversee employment at the LSF. All permanent employees at the LSF would be employed by and fall under the policies and protocols of institution B. Institution A would be involved in the hiring process and would provide input on performance evaluations. In some cases, supervision would be shared between the two institutions—for example, the director of the facility would report officially to institution B with some oversight shared by institution A. In turn, because the LSF was built on institution A's property, that institution agreed to handle all technology and information networks as well as building management and security for the facility. We thought that costs would balance out and that each institution would be equitably charged a fee for services.

Both institutions agreed to six permanent staff members for the LSF. The six would include a director, an operations manager, and four associates. It was decided that initially the director would be a librarian responsible for the overall management of the facility as well as for building relationships with both institutions to expand collaborations in collections development and management and services. The operations manager would train and supervise associates and ensure that the archive module operates efficiently and that services meet the expectations of users across both campuses. The four associates would be responsible for delivery, retrieval, systems inventory, and interlibrary loan. To date there are also plans to add a service manager, but this position is on hold as we move into the first year of operations. Currently, institution A has services staff and felt they could take on the work with existing staff. Institution B has moved 95 percent of its collections to the LSF, so although excellent service is of the utmost importance to both institutions, such service is particularly necessary for institution B, given that the core of its materials are located at the LSF.

TECHNOLOGY

With institution B taking on responsibility for all staffing in the LSF, institution A will have responsibility for technology because the infrastructure is already available on the property. Institution A outlined equipment needs along with the installation and configuration of hardware and software to support the LSF. Primary to moving forward was the selection of an inventory control system to secure materials and to have the best possible item tracking for effective and efficient storage facility management. The LSF steering committee considered two primary vendors and requested proposals. After checking references with other institutions and participating in our own proposal and review process, the steering committee decided to select a lesser known vendor to facilitate an accelerated ingest process to move materials from each of the libraries and ingest materials to the LSF. The chosen vendor's inventory software was flexible and had the necessary functionality to meet our requirements. The vendor was also willing to work on any adjustments that were needed. Other needs for technology included authentication, storage, wireless (network), and audiovisual services. A service-level agreement was developed to outline needs and requirements.

DISCOVERY

In the spring of 2014, institution A began preparation for migration to a next-generation library management solution. The "go live" date for the new platform was December 2015. During the summer of 2015, institution B decided to spearhead the migration of the state's integrated library system and move to the same library management solution. Institution B would be the first within the state's library system to adopt the new library management solution, but the accelerated move would expedite resource sharing between institutions A and B. At this time, only materials located in the LSF and tracked in the inventory system are discoverable through each of the two discovery systems for both institutions. There are challenges with full disclosure of holdings and materials across institutions for all materials, but upcoming development of the system will, it is hoped, improve access in the next year. The accelerated move of institution B to the new system in alignment with institution A was a huge undertaking, but it was a tremendous step toward enhanced access and the provision of a shared collection for both campuses.

ACCELERATED INGEST AND STANDARD OPERATIONS

With the LSF completed and furnished in November 2015, we initiated accelerated ingest for the facility. To oversee operations and ingest for the entire move, an internal employee from institution B was identified as manager of ingest and operations. The manager had deep knowledge of institution B's collections and an awareness of institution A's collections because of heavy involvement in the development of the planograph for the facility. Having internal staff involved in the new operation was extremely important not only in monitoring the activities related to the move but also in developing standard operating procedures (SOP) for all processes that would be used going forward. Each of the relevant working groups was involved in the SOP development process.

Ingest began with materials from institution A's museum storage in December 2015 and was completed in January 2016. We then ingested materials from institution B until April 2016. In April we began moving materials again from institution A, completing the relocation in July 2016. The last materials moved were from institution B. Ingest was officially completed in August 2016. Upon completion there were approximately 1,629,000 volumes located in the facility. During the ingest process we endured a considerable number of challenges that came mainly from materials deemed unfit for shelving and materials without barcodes. To work on these materials, each institution assigned existing staff from each of the campuses to the LSF to sort through the materials. This action kept the ingest work focused using the committed permanent staff and project staff.

Over the eight-month period, we hired an operations manager and four associates dedicated to the LSF. Hiring the LSF director has been challenging. In fact, the position has been posted three times. Most recently we adjusted the position description to expand the position's responsibility for building the collaboration in hopes of attracting more interested applicants. The director will oversee the LSF but will also work between the two libraries. In the meantime, we have activated the LSF management group composed of library leadership from the respective institutions as well as members of the ongoing subcommittees focused on technology, communications, collections, and preservation.

FUTURE AREAS OF COLLABORATION

With the LSF complete and work moving forward on the shared collection, we are now exploring further areas of collaboration. Some areas identified include cataloging; joint staffing; further development of the discovery system, especially regarding the development of a virtual browse; and digital repository services. In the fall of 2016, the LSF management group met monthly, continuing to oversee the joint management of the collaborative activities and the LSF. A website has been established to promote the LSF and to guide users with services offered. We are now focused on providing the best possible services and expanding access to resources. We also continue to explore collaborative collection development.

In regard to electronic resources, as previously mentioned there are significant impediments to realizing a shared vision due to copyright restrictions on digital collections. Both institutions have agreed to explore possibilities for collaborative negotiation for licenses. Exploration began with new subscriptions, but a broader strategy is being developed for the new subscriptions and renewals. In regard to licensing, the initial strategy was to license contracts under the umbrella of AB Inc., but general counsel at institution A recommended joint negotiation with each institution whereby each signs its respective licenses due to liability and the complexity of AB Inc.'s not having already established authorized users. Another strategy for working with publishers that both institutions are exploring is increasing the ability to restrict use of selected databases to a subset of the campus community. The goal is to be able to purchase subscriptions for smaller numbers of faculty and students. This approach is a strong possibility if both institutions can effectively manage these restrictions.

CONCLUSION

As previously stated, the enhanced collaboration has allowed both institutions to leverage expertise and resources. By effectively working together, the institutions have brought the project to a successful close. There still are numerous challenges, and there were many areas along the way where we did not agree initially but were able to openly communicate to reach workable solutions and compromise. We mutually benefited through shared expertise and resources in many areas. We investigated options in unison and moved forward with each detail, from the temperature and relative humidity of the archive module to the creation of requirements for the intake room. We thoughtfully addressed present-day needs but also anticipated future needs, operations, and even new partners. Management compromises for staffing created the best possible environment for the employees permanently located at the LSF, and we are taking advantage of the current campus services and technology in place to evenly distribute core operational needs. With the development of this collaboration, we have also established deeper engagement and relationships. We have acknowledged expertise and compromised when needed to increase value in the resources and services that we are able to offer to the faculty and students across both campuses. As we move into regular operations, we look now to new possibilities to serve our missions and expand our success.

AMY HARRIS HOUK and
KATHRYN M. CROWE

5

Form Follows Function

Creating a New Liaison Service Model

ACADEMIC LIBRARIES IN THE UNITED STATES have traditionally appointed liaisons or subject specialists to work with academic departments in building collections, providing information literacy instruction, and serving as a communication link between the library and the academic programs. In recent years, academic libraries have begun employing new, less staff-intensive methods, such as demand-driven acquisitions to build collections, and increasing their emphasis on special collections, information literacy, student learning, and access to discovery of information. These developments are evidenced in the "Ithaka S+R U.S. Library Survey 2013" of nearly five hundred library leaders and other published studies.[1] Library liaisons' roles have changed their foci from serving as selectors and staffing reference desks to collaborating with faculty on research and curriculum, working with faculty on scholarly communications problems, and generally being more engaged on campus. Furthermore, academic libraries are serving as important learning spaces on campus by providing a wide variety of group and individual spaces, technologies, and services. Many are hosting not only library services but also other student learning needs such as writing centers, media labs, and tutoring.

These developments in academic librarianship along with local changes provided the impetus to examine the roles of liaisons at the University Libraries (the Libraries) at the University of North Carolina at Greensboro. This case study will discuss the issues that sparked change, the process by which the changes occurred, and the status of liaison services today.

CONTEXT

The University of North Carolina at Greensboro (UNCG) is the sixth-largest school in the University of North Carolina system.[2] The Carnegie classification is R2 (higher research activity).[3] The University Libraries at UNCG consist of the large main Jackson Library and the Harold Schiffman Music Library, located in the School of Music building. The Libraries offer a print collection of over one million volumes, e-book offerings of over 800,000, and access to over 100,000 e-journals. The Libraries have ninety faculty and staff; librarians have faculty status and earn tenure. The University Libraries have had subject liaisons to academic departments for over twenty years. When the program was established in the early 1990s, the primary emphases were collection management in a print-based world, provision of a communication link between the Libraries and the academic departments, and library instruction. Most liaisons were located in Reference and Instructional Services (RIS). In addition to their collection management duties, liaisons spent between twelve and fifteen hours a week staffing the reference desk and provided course-integrated instruction sessions. A few librarians from departments outside RIS also served as liaisons to departments that needed little instructional support and primarily collection management support. The Libraries had an approval plan that brought in the majority of titles in the collection, but liaisons still spent approximately ten to fifteen hours a month working with faculty to select materials from annual budget allocations for each academic program. As online resources became more prevalent, liaisons began evaluating them to determine which ones to purchase. When there were weeding or storage transfer projects, liaisons determined whether collections would be retained. Liaisons also evaluated gift books in their liaison areas for possible inclusion in the collection. All liaisons were on the Collection Management Committee (CMC), which met once a month with the assistant dean for collections, who served as the chair. The liaisons in RIS reported to the head of reference who supervised their teaching, outreach, and public service work; she did not, however, supervise their collection management responsibilities.

Over the years as academic librarianship changed, liaisons at UNCG took on additional responsibilities. Information literacy instruction grew dramatically with a 126 percent increase between 2003 and 2008 and an additional

18 percent increase between 2008 and 2012. Liaisons became increasingly embedded into their academic departments and were providing more individual and small-group consultations, nearly doubling between 2008 and 2012. Liaisons also expanded outreach efforts to include working with learning communities and student organizations. As online learning and the "flipped classroom" concept took hold, liaisons began developing tutorials and other learning objects. Developments regarding new publishing models, data management, and scholarly communication also added expectations for liaisons to increase their awareness of these developments and work with faculty on them. Because these new obligations came on top of the traditional ones, liaisons were frustrated and overburdened. Although most were doing fewer reference desk hours, many wanted to devote even more time to promoting information literacy and working closely with students and faculty on their research projects. Several weeding projects required time-consuming and tedious title-by-title examination of collections, resulting in what was labeled "spreadsheet fatigue." Many liaisons wanted to spend less time doing book selection. Also, the CMC structure had become unwieldy, and many felt the meetings unproductive.

The Libraries' strategic plan for 2012–13 called for a holistic look at the service desk configuration and an examination of the Libraries' organizational structure, as depicted in figure 5.1. As part of this review, the library administration wanted liaisons to spend less time working at the reference desk and doing collection management tasks in order to focus on promoting information literacy and working with faculty on scholarly communications and research activities. As in many academic libraries, the quantity of reference questions had dropped 54 percent between 2007 and 2012. The Libraries joined the Scholarly Publishing and Academic Resources Coalition (SPARC) in 2008 and wanted to be actively involved with new developments in open access and author rights and share these developments with faculty. In 2013 new data management requirements from funding agencies created an opportunity for liaison librarians to work with faculty who needed assistance creating data management plans. The Libraries had established an institutional repository in 2007 and needed to more actively recruit faculty to deposit their publications. Librarians and library administration also sought to refine the Libraries' collection management operations to ensure that they were purchasing what our community needed in the most efficient and cost-effective manner possible. New purchasing models, such as patron-driven acquisitions, were available that could save staff time as well. These changes to the way the Libraries acquired materials necessitated an examination of the approval plan and the way monies were allocated and budgeted to build collections for each academic unit.

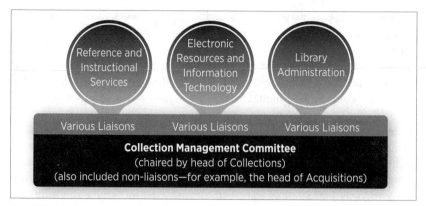

FIGURE 5.1
Old organizational structure

LIAISON TASK FORCE APPOINTED

With the convergence of all these factors, the dean of the Libraries appointed a task force in early 2012 to examine how much time was spent on collection development. The charge was as follows:

> The enhanced responsibilities of our liaisons have created some very real problems regarding the amount of time that can be spent on collection development. As new responsibilities emerge and the way in which we handle collection development has changed, it is time to examine how we are organized to manage all of these competing responsibilities. To that end, this task force is charged to: 1. Define the collection development, instruction, outreach, and newly defined and enhanced responsibilities of our liaisons. 2. Define the ways that collection development has changed over the years. 3. Benchmark with other libraries to see how they are handling the complexities of liaison responsibilities in new, creative, and innovative ways. 4. Recommend an organizational model for collection development and other liaison responsibilities that will allow us to give the proper attention to both areas in a sleek and efficient way. More than one organizational model should be recommended providing alternatives to choose from. The task force is encouraged to consult/talk with others in the Libraries and to consider focus group interactions with academic faculty members in order to provide more voices to the final report of the Liaison Collections Responsibilities Task Force.[4]

After a summer strategic planning retreat, library administration amended the charge somewhat to change the focus from collections to public service while still examining all aspects of liaison work. The task force consisted of three librarians from RIS, the electronic resources librarian, and the assistant dean for administrative services. This group began by creating a list of the current responsibilities of liaisons in the following six areas:

1. Teaching
2. Research support and consulting
3. Outreach and promotion
4. Collections
5. Scholarly communication
6. Professional development

The task force's next step was to document the strengths and weaknesses of the existing model. The strengths included the relationships built between faculty and librarians and the liaisons' ability to focus on the aspects of the work that were most interesting to them. The weaknesses of the existing model included the absence of a holistic supervisory structure for the liaison program, the need for all liaisons to be skilled at all areas of liaison work, and the lack of prioritization of academic departments based on need. The task force members shared a draft of the responsibilities document as well as the strengths and weaknesses with liaisons to gain their feedback.

After this introductory work was completed, the group moved on to benchmarking other libraries. The task force members searched the library literature but could not find any articles discussing academic libraries that had successfully changed their liaison model. Google searches were more fruitful and led the group to Villanova University, Johns Hopkins University, the University of Guelph, and Utah State University. The group contacted librarians at each of these institutions for details about their respective liaison models.

The liaison model at Falvey Memorial Library at Villanova consisted of an academic integration department with seven subject teams, a department head, functional coordinators (an instructional services coordinator and a collection development coordinator), and staff. The department head and functional coordinators served as a leadership team, setting departmental goals, providing professional development opportunities for liaisons, and assisting the subject teams as needed. The library's reference services were transitioned to an interdepartmental information and research assistance team.

Johns Hopkins University Libraries had an academic liaisons department with a head and functional coordinators. However, not all liaisons were in this department. The libraries provided monthly professional development opportunities attended by most liaisons.

The library at the University of Guelph consisted entirely of functional teams. Traditional liaison functions were divided among several teams, including information resources (collection management), learning and curriculum support (library instruction), and research and scholarship (research support).

Utah State University had a decentralized model, with four functional coordinators and subject teams, but no liaison department. Instead, liaisons were housed in various departments.

The task force also met with colleagues at Wake Forest University and the University of North Carolina at Chapel Hill to discuss the responsibilities of and the challenges facing liaison librarians at their respective institutions.

RECOMMENDATIONS FROM THE TASK FORCE

After gathering this information, the task force drafted a report to the dean that included the three following options and recommendations to create new departmental models: a collections department model, a subject team model, and a functional team model. Each recommendation could be enacted individually or in combination with one or more of the other models.

The collections department model came primarily from the benchmarking process when the task force learned that most academic libraries have a collections department. The proposed collections department would consist of a collections coordinator or department head reporting to the assistant dean of Collections and Technical Services. The department would have at least one staff member and student workers. This department would complete tasks such as title-by-title ordering and weeding, approval plan maintenance, collecting use statistics, and communicating with vendors. This department would reduce the amount of time liaisons spend on collections-related work—one of the main reasons liaisons were interested in exploring other models—and allow them to spend more time on teaching and consultations.

The subject team model would create a new liaison department and three subject teams: humanities, social sciences, and natural sciences. Each team would be made up of librarians with relevant disciplinary expertise and be led by a subject team coordinator. All full-time liaisons would be part of a liaison department whose head would report directly to the associate dean for public services. These full-time liaisons would work with the academic departments having the greatest need for public service engagement—namely, teaching and research consultations. Part-time liaisons could serve as liaisons to departments with limited public service needs or be co-liaisons to an active department along with a full-time liaison. The leadership team would consist of the department head, subject team leaders, and functional coordinators, which could include an instruction coordinator, collections coordinator, and other coordinators, depending on the needs of the liaisons at a given time. The coordinators would also be full-time liaisons. Within each subject team, members would set goals and work together to meet the needs of their faculty and students. Each team would have a staff person who would assist the liaisons.

The functional team model, inspired by the University of Guelph, would be the most radical change from the existing liaison model. This model would eliminate the departmental liaison structure entirely and replace it with functional teams such as scholarly communications, first-year instruction, and instructional technology. Teaching faculty who have needs in a specific area would be directed to the appropriate functional team as opposed to having one point of contact for all library needs. Librarians would be placed in functional teams based on their expertise, and additional training would be required.

The task force further recommended a time line for implementing the new structure over a two-year period beginning in summer 2013.

IMPLEMENTATION

The task force submitted its final report to the dean in September 2012.[5] The Libraries' leadership reviewed the report and brought recommendations to the broader administrative advisory group, which includes all department heads. After discussion and vetting among the Libraries' leadership and the liaisons, a hybrid form of the recommendations was adopted. It was decided to transition to a team structure that includes subject and functional teams (figure 5.2). Three subject or disciplinary teams (humanities, social sciences,

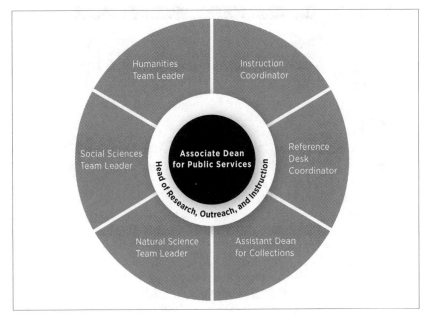

FIGURE 5.2
New organizational structure

and natural sciences) and four functional teams (collections, scholarly communication, instruction, and reference desk) were established. The subject teams include liaisons from RIS and the Schiffman Music Library as well as special collections and university archives (SCUA). Each subject team has a representative on each functional team. The functional teams include liaisons and other appropriate staff and librarians from technical services, electronic resources, and RIS. The teams are coordinated by the head of reference and instructional services with a dotted line to the associate dean for public services. Although administration did not establish a collections department, much of the collections work was transferred to the existing Technical Services Department.

The dean of the Libraries agreed to the two-year implementation time line recommended by the task force (figures 5.3 and 5.4). The process began in winter and spring of 2013 with evidence gathering. Liaisons tracked their tasks and workloads through a survey, and the results were discussed. In the summer of 2013 the implementation process began with training of the liaisons on how to work in teams. A faculty member in the Communication Studies Department with expertise in team building conducted a workshop for

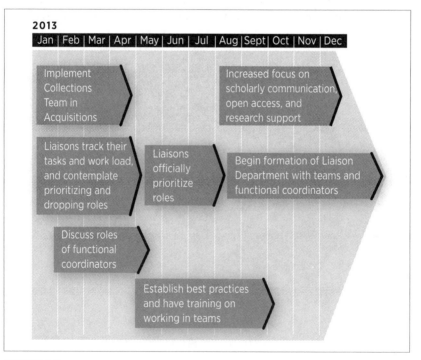

FIGURE 5.3

Planning and implementation time line 2013

team members about small-group and team communication. This presentation detailed best practices for creating successful groups, holding productive meetings, and setting group goals. At the conclusion of the training session, the teams met to begin thinking about initial goals for the upcoming year.

The next activities were to compile the information gathered by liaisons about their current workload and have further discussions about how they wanted to see their roles change in the future. The major findings included the following:

1. Most liaisons spent the most time on teaching and consulting.

2. Most liaisons reported that teaching and consulting are also the highest priorities of liaison work for most academic departments.

3. Many liaisons would like to have more time for outreach activities.

4. There was wide, but not universal, interest among liaisons in dropping title-by-title selection, especially the requirement of fully expending their respective book budgets at the end of the fiscal year.

5. A significant number of liaisons believed that specialists rather than the liaisons themselves should be responsible for scholarly communications outreach and training.

6. There was some concern about the quality of service because liaisons were spending less time on the reference desk.

7. Liaisons believed that they were becoming increasingly embedded in the academic departments; the liaisons with larger embedded roles reported spending the most time on consultations.

The liaisons presented and discussed the results in a meeting that helped the administration decide how to move forward. The teams used this information and their initial goals to create a plan for the year. The team leaders met with the head of RIS to establish goals for the whole liaison program.

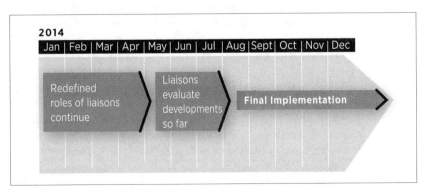

FIGURE 5.4

Planning and implementation time line 2014

After the goals were set, the liaison teams began implementing them. Several subject teams engaged in curriculum mapping in order to target appropriate courses for information literacy instruction. Continuing education opportunities were greatly enhanced, primarily through peer training and webinars. Although there were more meetings, most felt that those meetings were more productive. Collection management procedures were refined with staff in the Technical Services Department taking on more responsibilities. The instruction team provided several training sessions that were open to all members of liaison teams instead of only to full-time liaisons, as they had been previously. The instruction team also developed a tool kit for providing information literacy instruction to online classes. Members of the scholarly communications team researched the needs for data management on campus and developed and marketed a LibGuide, a set of web pages for research assistance, to the faculty. The desk team adopted a model more like triage, and paraprofessional staff took on desk scheduling. Librarians continued to staff the desk but most worked only two to four hours per week.

Subject teams also offered professional development related to their subject areas. The humanities team offered training on ArtStor, a resource that provides nearly two million digital images in the arts, architecture, the humanities, and the sciences, and the social sciences team provided training on using Scopus (a tool primarily used for science, technology, engineering, and medical research) for social sciences research. The humanities and social sciences team held a joint training session on the Association of Religion Data Archives, a freely available archive. The science team offered training on new science databases available to the Libraries through our statewide consortium. All the training sessions were open to all members of liaison teams. Some of the ideas for the training sessions were brainstormed at the beginning of the year during the goal-setting process, and others were suggested by members of other teams based on needs they determined through their work.

After the first year, all the new teams held a daylong retreat to evaluate the new structure. Several breakout sessions were held throughout the day followed by reports to the entire group. At the end of the day, the consensus was that the new structure was working well, that much had been accomplished, and that some refinements and improvements were needed going forward.

The teams recommended that RIS be renamed Research, Outreach, and Instruction (ROI) to more accurately reflect the department's mission. The name change was implemented after approval from the Libraries' administrative advisory group. Despite the fact that the new organization was working well, challenges remained largely because there were not clear lines of reporting for every team, resulting in a "messy" structure. Although most liaisons felt that communication among liaisons as well as between liaisons and administration was vastly improved, there were still gaps. Some librarians had concerns about the new model—namely, a potential decrease in service quality at a reference desk staffed mostly by students and staff, and concern about ordering and weeding being handled by staff.

It was also important to communicate the reorganization to the entire library staff. To address this need, liaisons, led by the head of RIS, held an open house at the end of the first year of implementation. Team members were available at tables to answer questions and share information. After listening to a few introductory remarks, staff could move from table to table to learn more about each team. Prizes and refreshments were included to make the open house fun!

To increase communication among themselves, liaisons decided to hold monthly "coffee klatches" in order to provide more interaction across the teams. These coffee klatches were designed to be opportunities for discussion among liaisons, as opposed to the training sessions. The discussion topics could be proposed by a team or an individual liaison. Topics included liaison accomplishments, transfer students and information literacy, and high-impact practices. As a result of these discussions, an overall goal for the liaison program was established:

> Our mission is to partner with students, faculty and staff to enhance teaching, research and learning and to support the overall mission, values and goals of UNCG Libraries.[6]

The new assistant dean for collections and scholarly communication had been appointed during the first year, and her goal was to continue to refine collections planning and expand scholarly communications efforts. The subject and functional teams agreed to continue offering professional development opportunities for liaisons.

Over the second year, the teams continued to refine their operations. One improvement to the team structure was that librarians from departments other than ROI became more involved with information literacy, outreach, and scholarly communication efforts. SCUA had greatly increased its number of instruction sessions. The Libraries had also established a digital media commons in 2012, and that unit was providing a great deal of instruction and faculty development. The music librarian was heavily embedded in the curriculum, but because she was in another building, she had not always been a part of conversations. The team structure provided more opportunities for librarians to learn what others were doing and to collaborate with each other. These new partnerships also enabled liaisons to engage with faculty in new ways that benefited student learning. One example was a partnership between the history liaison, SCUA librarians, and a history professor to provide information literacy instruction for an undergraduate capstone course and a graduate-level course on teaching at the college level. An assessment of the bibliographies was conducted for the undergraduate capstone course, indicating that students who scheduled a consultation with the librarian scored better than those who did not.

Another step for the new program was to develop an updated document that defined the roles of liaisons. It was necessary to codify liaison roles so that current liaisons would have a guide. In addition, the document would serve as a mechanism to market to faculty so that they would understand what services were available to them. In addition, the document would be useful for recruiting and training new librarians—prospective candidates would know what was expected of them. The associate dean for public services put together a small group to develop this document. A draft was reviewed by all liaisons and, after revisions were submitted and approved by the Libraries' administration, the guide is now easily accessible online.[7]

One problem that had gone unresolved under the previous organizational structure was how to redistribute a liaison's areas when a liaison left the organization. Typically, another person was hired to cover the vacant areas instead of looking critically at all the needs of the liaison program. With the new liaison structure, the teams could work together to assess the areas of greatest need. In late 2015, when a liaison with a large number of social sciences liaison areas retired, the social sciences team developed a proposal to redistribute most of the subject areas to existing liaisons, as opposed to hiring a new librarian to work with those departments. As a result of this vacant librarian line, the social sciences team proposed that the Libraries hire an additional first-year instruction librarian with a limited number of liaison areas, due to the high volume of classes in the first-year information literacy program. The team saw this area as being of greater need. The proposal was approved.

Librarians at UNCG have been honored to present on the reorganization several times, including at the Charleston Conference and the Association of College and Research Libraries Conference.[8] They have also shared our experience with librarians who are interested in reorganizing their liaison structure by visiting other libraries or hosting librarians at UNCG.

FUTURE PLANS

As the liaison teams move forward, the Libraries will continue to examine and refine the team structure. Recent retirements and new hires have provided the opportunity to make tweaks, and more opportunities will arise. It is important to continuously focus goals and measures to make sure they align with the goals of the Libraries and the university. Providing ongoing training and professional development opportunities is essential so that liaisons remain current. Furthermore, the liaison librarians need to communicate and publicize how their work benefits the campus. Collections planning will be important to ensure that the Libraries provide the best resources possible within constrained budgets. Library administration also plans to refine our performance evaluation process for liaisons.

LESSONS LEARNED

Overall, the methodical process of researching, choosing, and implementing a new liaison model was a success. However, given the opportunity to do it over again, we could have done some things differently. Although the process was very participatory, the task force should have invited more input from our paraprofessional staff. Although they do not serve as liaisons, many paraprofessionals are involved in the work of the teams, and their input would have been useful. Similarly, it would have been valuable to bring in an outside perspective from librarians in other library departments who are not liaisons but who interact with teaching faculty. In addition, enhanced communication with the entire library staff about the process would have kept everyone in the loop and prevented misconceptions about the intent and goals of the reorganization.

Concerns with the new model itself were largely allayed once it was implemented. One concern mentioned in the liaison survey was a potential decrease in service quality at the reference desk if liaisons spent less time staffing it. In fact, the restructuring enabled liaisons who enjoyed desk work to spend more time there while other liaisons focused on consultations and information literacy instruction.

RECOMMENDATIONS

It was fortunate that the motivation and impetus to reorganize came from the bottom up as well as the top down. It is not often that this synergy occurs! Change is difficult and needs to be an inclusive process. This reorganization was successful both in process and outcome. By encouraging librarians to develop close ties with faculty and students, the new liaison structure allows librarians to take the library to the students and faculty, both in person and electronically. Working with librarians who fully understand disciplinary conventions and research priorities is an effective way to facilitate student learning and faculty research. Libraries that are considering restructuring their liaisons need to be sure to have buy-in and participation among the liaisons, their supervisors, and library administration. Another reason this restructuring went so well was the fact that the process was participatory at all levels. It is also essential to align with library and university goals and outcomes. And you can never communicate too much. Be sure to tell your story and celebrate your success!

NOTES

1. Roger C. Schonfeld and Matthew P. Long, "Ithaka S+R U.S. Library Survey 2013" (March 11, 2014), www.sr.ithaka.org/research-publications/ithaka-sr-us-library-survey-2013.

2. National Center for Education Statistics, IPEDS (Integrated Postsecondary Education Data System), "Reported Full-Time Equivalent Undergraduate Enrollment, 2013–14," http://nces.ed.gov/ipeds/.

3. Carnegie Classification of Institutions of Higher Education, "University of North Carolina at Greensboro," http://carnegieclassifications.iu.edu/index.php.

4. University of North Carolina at Greensboro, Committees, Groups, Task Forces, and Projects, "Liaison Collections Responsibilities Task Force," http://libshare .uncg.edu/sites/bts/CGTP/Pages/ltf.aspx.

5. University of North Carolina at Greensboro, Liaison Collections Responsibilities Task Force, "Final Report of the Liaison Collections Responsibilities Task Force" (2012), http://libres.uncg.edu/ir/uncg/listing.aspx?id=16443.

6. University of North Carolina at Greensboro, University Libraries, "Liaisons Group Mission," http://libshare.uncg.edu/sites/bts/CGTP/LTDocuments/ LiaisonsGroupMissionandobjectives2013final.htm.

7. University of North Carolina at Greensboro, University Libraries, "Liaison Roles and Responsibilities" (2015), http://library.uncg.edu/info/library_liaison _responsibilities.aspx.

8. Steve M. Cramer, Beth R. Bernhardt, Mike A. Crumpton, Amy L. Harris, and Nancy B. Ryckman, "Great Expectations: New Organizational Models for Overworked Liaisons Based on the UNCG Libraries Liaison Collections Responsibilities Task Force," *Proceedings of the Charleston Library Conference* (2012), http://dx.doi.org/10.5703/1288284315112.

LISA O'HARA
and LES MOOR

6

Using a Project Management Methodology to Reorganize Technical Services

THIS CASE STUDY FOCUSES on the use of project management methodology in library reorganization to foster staff participation and decision making. In 2014 the management team of the Technical Services Department recognized that reorganization was necessary to manage the workload associated with electronic resources more efficiently and effectively. To ensure that the reorganization was successful, the management team employed a project management methodology that would allow the decision making for the project to be driven mainly by the staff employed in Technical Services. This approach meant that the business case was laid out early in the project, a very clear objective was set, and working groups were established to achieve the objective. During the project, all staff in Technical Services were involved in the decision making and were members of one of the working groups, ensuring that the project was inclusive and that the staff performing the work were able to create the workflows necessary to reach the objective. Milestones were negotiated with the management team, the reorganization happened on time, and Technical Services reached the stated objective.

The university is a medium-sized, research-intensive institution with approximately 29,000 students and 8,700 faculty and staff, including approximately one hundred library support staff and fifty-five librarians with faculty status. There are eighteen libraries (the Libraries) across two campuses and a number of satellite locations. Technical Services (TS) is a centralized unit serving these libraries and reports to the associate university librarian for collections.

The TS Department has experienced many changes since the mid-1990s as more and more content has become available in electronic format. However, the staffing did not change at the same pace, and many people working in the department had been hired to catalog print monographs or to receive print serials. Gradually over the years, the work distribution among the staff became uneven; staff who worked with electronic resources were unable to keep pace with the workload whereas some staff who worked on print materials had light workloads and hence were underutilized. A series of events brought this situation to a crisis point: first, more staff who were working with electronic resources left their positions (through transfers to other departments, resignations, or retirements) than did staff working with print. Furthermore, positions were frequently left unfilled due to budgetary constraints. These circumstances eventually led to a situation in which only three staff members with electronic resources expertise remained while eight staff members worked predominantly with print. Next, one of the three remaining electronic resources people suffered an extended illness leaving only two, and shortly thereafter one of those two submitted her resignation to take a professional position at another university. In response, the head of TS and the head of Discovery and Delivery Services (DDS) began to work on a reorganization of the department in 2015, with the approval of the university librarian.

CREATING A NEW ORGANIZATIONAL MODEL

The Technical Services management team—comprised of the head of TS, the head of DDS, the three TS librarians, and the department's two supervisors—held a series of meetings during which team members conceived a new organizational model by examining the specific processes that would be carried out by each team. The management team had two primary objectives in constructing a new organizational model: first, to more evenly distribute work among the staff in the department (specifically electronic resources work, which was the most unevenly distributed), and second, to ensure that we did not create knowledge or skill silos. Multiple staff would be tasked with doing high-volume and mission-critical work so that the department would be positioned to respond nimbly to high-priority work and unexpected situations by having a cadre of staff who knew how to do any particular task and who could be redirected to other tasks as work ebbed and flowed in the department. A secondary objective was to increase job satisfaction for all TS staff.

This new model replaced the Monographs and Serials units, each of which had a supervisor, and created four new teams. Each staff member would now serve simultaneously on at least two teams, dividing time between them according to the needs of each team. For example, a single staff member during the month of April might be assigned to monograph receiving on one team and to electronic resources licensing on another team. This person would monitor the workload in each of those tasks and divide the time as needed to keep on top of the work in both areas. The following month that staff member would be assigned to different areas on each team, and someone else would take over the monograph receiving and electronic resources licensing. This structure made the department nimbler: every staff member would become knowledgeable in at least two broad areas, providing a pool of skilled staff who could be assigned and reassigned as needed.

The four new teams and their areas of responsibility are outlined as follows:

> **Electronic Resource Setup:** This team arranges trials of new electronic resources, compiles and makes available use statistics for electronic resources, handles all support staff–level work related to electronic resources licensing including "license lifts" (temporary expansions or suspensions of simultaneous user limits for specific electronic resources in order to support special events during which the resources will be used intensively), and manages the Libraries' LibGuides and the A–Z list of databases and other electronic resources collections.

> **Subscription Management:** This team receives all incoming electronic resources trouble reports and resolves or routes these problems as needed, records any post-subscription perpetual access rights that we may have to our electronic resources, handles transfers of electronic resources between publishers, manages the subscription renewal process, reconciles vendors' lists of our licensed resources against our own list to ensure that they remain in sync, and handles any serial cancellations.

> **Receiving and Metadata:** This team does all the cataloging and catalog maintenance work and will provide metadata support for digital collections throughout the university as more of that work comes to TS. This team also receives new library materials and processes claims for missing issues of print serials.

> **Ordering and Activations:** This team orders new monographs and initiates new subscriptions (for print and electronic versions), activates electronic resources in our discovery layer, and

obtains pricing for monographs and subscriptions in response to requests from public services staff.

The two finance staff members, who worked outside the former Monographs and Serials units, were not affected by the reorganization.

The next step was to assign existing staff members to the new teams. After estimating how many staff members each team would need, the head of Technical Services scheduled an all-staff meeting to discuss the upcoming reorganization—why it was necessary, what it would achieve, and how it would be accomplished (the project). At this meeting the head of Technical Services showed staff the new teams and briefly discussed their respective responsibilities. Staff were told that everyone would have to work on two teams and were asked to think about which ones they would like to be assigned to. This meeting was followed up with a survey on which each staff member ranked the four teams in order of preference.

The results of this survey were not surprising: almost everyone ranked highest those teams whose work most closely resembled the work they already did. The staff on the Monographs team almost universally selected Receiving and Metadata along with Ordering and Activations, while the staff in Serials overwhelmingly selected Electronic Resource Setup and Subscription Management. If everyone had been given their first and second choice, the structure of the department would have been relatively unchanged: workload would have remained unevenly distributed, and electronic resources knowledge and skills would have remained siloed in a relatively small number of staff.

Because the electronic resources work was most in need of more staff and because none of the people who weren't already doing it indicated an interest, the TS management team realized that we would have to impose this work on staff who weren't already doing it (i.e., members of the Monographs team). After considerable discussion, we decided that the fairest way to do this would be to require all members of the Monographs team to take on some electronic resources work. However, another objective of the reorganization was to improve job satisfaction, and taking Monographs people away from the work they liked and replacing it with work they weren't interested in did not seem a promising way to achieve this goal.

Thus, two objectives of the reorganization (a more even distribution of work and improvement of job satisfaction) were in conflict. After more discussion, we decided to assign everyone on the Monographs team to the new team that they ranked highest (which was either Receiving and Metadata or Ordering and Activations) but also assign them to one of the electronic resources–intensive teams (Electronic Resource Setup or Subscription Management). This approach meant that the staff on the Monographs team would continue to do the work they liked best but also had to learn the work of one of the electronic resources–intensive teams. The staff on the Serials team were more likely to get their first and second choices because they were already working in electronic resources–intensive areas that had the greatest staffing need.

Finally, with the decisions made about what the new organizational model would look like, we were ready to make the move to the new organizational structure. Because the head of DDS had recently completed certification in PRINCE2 (Projects in Controlled Environments) Project Management, we decided to use that method for implementation of the new organizational structure. We felt that the methodology was suitable for this project because it defined tasks and time lines and allowed us to manage the project in clearly understood stages.

PROJECT MANAGEMENT METHODOLOGY

PRINCE2 is a project management method used by the Office of Government Commerce (OGC) in the United Kingdom.[1] It was adopted at the university in the Information Technology Office (ITO), and there were opportunities for staff outside the ITO who work closely with ITO staff to take the training and receive certification at the Foundation level, the basic level at which users are introduced to the management method, its principles, themes, and terminology. The certification involves a two-day course with an exam on which a score of 80 percent or better is required.

The TS project was considered in PRINCE2 terms to be low risk, low cost, and confined to a single site, so it was set up as a simple project, meaning it would follow the PRINCE2 principles but would not have the same organization as a large-scale project. The PRINCE2 principles include continued business justification, learning from experience, setting up defined roles and responsibilities, managing by stages, managing by exception, focusing on products, and tailoring to suit the project environment. All these principles were applied to the TS project.

PRINCE2 also defines seven themes (Business Case, Organization, Quality, Plans, Risk, Change, Progress) and seven processes (Starting Up a Project, Directing a Project, Initiating a Project, Controlling a Stage, Managing Product Delivery, Managing a Stage Boundary, Closing a Project). Because this was a simple project, some of the processes were combined, and the project was implemented in the following three phases.

PHASE 1

PRINCE2 Processes—Starting Up a Project, Directing a Project, and Initiating a Project (September–December 2014)

Most of the work of the project manager (PM) is done in these three phases, incorporating the themes outlined in the following sections.

Business Case

The business case for the project stated that Technical Services needed to move to the new organizational model to increase the staff's capacity to deal with high-priority and high-turnaround-time tasks. The objective (product) of the project was to triple the number of staff able to work with electronic resources tasks within TS by June 2015 through establishing new Technical Services teams. The TS management team believed that this approach would allow sufficient staff to meet the ebbs and flows of work in each of the various areas of the department as well as decrease the stress felt by staff working with electronic resources and increase job satisfaction for all TS staff. The PM continued to ensure that the objective was being considered in all phases of the project, in keeping with the PRINCE2 principles.

Organization

The Project Board (PB) in PRINCE2 is responsible for the overall direction of the project and is accountable for the success of the project. Normally a PB is made up of a senior user, an executive, and a senior supplier, but in this case, the PB consisted of only the head of DDS (the parent department of TS), who filled all three roles (because this was a simple project). It is the PB's responsibility to provide the authority for the project and to direct and control the project through the PM, who reports exceptions and asks for authorization for any changes to the project that are outside the tolerances as defined in the change theme.

The head of Technical Services served as the PM and was responsible for the day-to-day management of the project, reporting to the PB completions of stages and deviations that were outside the tolerances. A project management team (PMT) was created that consisted of the PM and the working group managers as well as the two supervisors in the department.

Working group manager roles were assigned by the PM to three librarians on the team based on the four new teams that were being established within TS. The managers' role was to plan the team meetings, keep the team on track, get everyone's involvement, follow up on decisions and action items, and plan for the next meeting. Each working group also assigned a recorder whose role was to record the important information, decisions, and action items and to send out the meeting highlights and actions. All staff who would later serve on the new TS team that the working group was creating became working group members. The working group members were responsible for participating in meetings and team activities. The reports of the meetings were shared with all members of the project through the project management software, Basecamp.

The following ground rules were eventually established by the PM and the teams:

We treat each other with respect.

We value constructive dialogue. We will avoid being defensive and give feedback in a constructive manner.

We come prepared to work at the meeting, having reviewed documents and thought processes.

We encourage "questions of clarification" and discourage "questions of attack."

We speak for ourselves only.

We speak up if something is not working for us personally.

We commit to team decisions and strategies.

We make decisions by consensus (all team members consent to a decision, but it does not have to be unanimous consent whereby everyone is *completely* satisfied with the decision).

Each working group was given the necessary resources to carry out its work. These resources ended up being scheduled time to carry out the reorganization tasks, facilities for providing training on the tasks, and meeting space. Although outside training could also have been provided, ultimately it was not needed.

Quality

The PM had a good understanding of the level of quality required for the project and performed quality assurance at each stage of the project.

Plans

The PM and PB wrote product descriptions for key deliverables as the mandate for each working group, and a schedule was created. The schedule involved setting dates for working group meetings and for key deliverables such as formulating training plans, writing procedures for tasks, having training done for the new TS teams, finalizing the procedures and training, and going live with the new organizational structure.

Risk

A formal analysis of the risks was not completed by the PM and PB as part of this project, although we considered the risks before the project was established, as discussed earlier in this chapter. The risks mainly were related to staff members themselves, and the main mitigation method was to involve them in the process as much as possible.

Change

In PRINCE2, a method of controlling changes to the project must be established. In this project, each working group would be allowed to make changes within the mandate of that working group, but broader changes affecting more than one working group would have to be agreed on by the PMT. The PB would have to be consulted if the change might affect the business case.

Progress

Progress was reported by the working groups through the minutes of each weekly meeting, which were available to all members of the project. The PMT met monthly to discuss progress, and any suggested changes affecting more than one working group were brought to that meeting to be agreed upon by the PMT. Although we didn't put any formal progress controls in place, the PMT held discussions monthly to monitor progress through each stage, detect problems and identify risks, and initiate corrective action. The PM informed the PB and authorized further work at each stage, ensuring that the business case was still valid. This process was far less formal in practice than described here because many of these steps were a natural part of the interactions of the staff involved who work together daily.

These processes took approximately 10 percent of the time of the head of Technical Services and the head of DDS. Because the work was done in a series of meetings spread out over three months, it was not the main focus of any one workday. The future members of the PMT were consulted, but the project was not a major part of their work at this time.

PHASE 2

PRINCE 2 Processes—Controlling a Stage, Managing Product Delivery, and Managing a Stage Boundary (January–August 2015)

Phase 2 processes involve assigning work to be done within the working groups themselves, monitoring the work, dealing with issues, and reporting progress to the PB. As in the previous processes, all the themes must be considered in each of these PRINCE2 processes.

In the TS project, these processes were managed by the PM's meeting with the PMT monthly and with the PB as needed, reflecting the PRINCE2 Organization theme.

The PM ensured that the work was progressing per the schedule (Plans and Progress themes), described as *stages,* and that each stage was completed before the next stage began. The PMT discussed any deviations (Change theme), which were then presented to the PB for authorization if necessary.

At the end of each stage, the PM discussed the stage with the PB, who then approved moving on to the next stage. The PM and PB also considered the business case in these meetings to make sure that there was a continued justification for the project (Business Case theme). Again, these processes were less formal than described here.

Working Group Dynamics

The PM attended all the initial meetings of each working group and continued to attend several other working group meetings during the project.

The groups had some members who were already experts in the domain of the team as well as some novices who knew very little about it. This combination produced a dynamic in which, during meetings in which decisions were being made about the activities of the future team, the experts dominated the discussion while the novices largely observed. This result was expected and ultimately somewhat helpful in that it gave the novices a chance to immerse themselves in the working of their new team before they were expected to understand it or make meaningful contributions. In addition, the combination of experts and novices created a situation in which fresh eyes scrutinized established practices, which sometimes had unexpected benefits.

For example, with so many staff about to learn new work, well-documented procedures would be critical and were a key deliverable of the project. However, given that the library management system had migrated to Alma the previous year and given the fact that procedures documentation had in many cases been previously neglected, many of our processes were poorly or incompletely documented. The experts on each team drafted these procedures, and during this process of having to examine and document a procedure in some detail, these team members frequently came to question procedures and workflows that the department had been doing a long time.

This challenge to existing practice led to considerable revision, typically to improve efficiency but also to move a procedure from one team to another where it was felt the procedure would be completed more readily. If a team member thought that a different team should perform a particular procedure, the team would discuss the move, and if there was consensus, the proposal was made to the target team (the team that should take on the work as proposed). This process was often informal because all the staff served on at least two working groups, so it was common for those deliberations to be reported to the other group by the staff who served on both working groups. This became an effective way to communicate and to problem solve as a group, because those members heard the discussions of both groups.

Another common occurrence took place when one group was trying to figure out the best way to handle a procedure that involved another group. At these times a group would typically invite one or more experts from the other group to its meetings so that they could work it out together. This approach proved very helpful and led to processes within a team that not only took into account the processes and needs of other teams within the department but also demonstrated that staff were striving for the best solution for the department rather than just what would be easiest for their own team.

After the planning and documentation stage, the project moved into the training stage, during which the team's new members learned the responsibilities of their new team. This stage took place over the course of about six months and produced the essential skills learning as well as a rigorous reviewing of the procedures documentation because someone who knew little about the process had to use the documentation to learn it. In this stage team members changed documentation frequently, adding things that were missing or revising instructions that the learners found confusing—and creating a few occasions on which the learners identified workflows that were inefficient and proposed changes. When this happened, the working group would discuss the existing workflow and the proposed changes, frequently accepting the proposal and revising the workflow and the documentation accordingly.

Another interesting group dynamic—and one that was uncomfortable—was what one of the group members early in the process dubbed *seepage*. The term *seepage* referred to a process with steps that fell into the domain of more than one team. In some cases, seepage would lead to handoffs at several points through the process from one team to another. Handoffs are undesirable because information must pass from one person to another, and every time this happens an opportunity for miscommunication arises, which can lead to error as well as delays in the work.

One example of a handoff is a database trial that leads to a decision to license it for the university. The trial request and setup are handled by the Electronic Resource Setup group, but if the library decides it wants to purchase the resource when the trial is completed, the Ordering and Activations (O&A) team obtains pricing while the Electronic Resource Setup group ensures that the license meets our needs and will negotiate any necessary changes with the vendor. Once the work of both groups is finished, O&A places the order and activates the resource when the purchase is complete. Finally, Electronic Resource Setup must add the resource to the A–Z list. All this used to be done by a single person in the old structure, and now bits of it could potentially be done by up to five people. This type of situation happened often enough to cause concern about the division of labor among the four teams. Did we divide the work in ways to provide efficient and quality service? Indeed, in some cases the handoffs seemed so frequent or so arbitrary that the groups ultimately moved steps from one team to another to reduce handoffs. Nevertheless, some processes have more handoffs now than they did before the reorganization.

Time Commitments

The members of the working groups spent at least 25 percent of their time on this project during this period because they were drafting documentation, training, and revising documentation as well as meeting weekly. The PM spent less time, approximately 10 percent of his time, during this phase on the project. The PB spent less than 5 percent of her time on the project during this phase.

PHASE 3

PRINCE2 Process—Closing a Project (August 2015)

The final process in PRINCE2 is Closing a Project, in which the objective is to verify that the project met its stated purpose, confirm that the products are acceptable, review performance, assess benefits, and ensure that all risks have been addressed or provisions have been made to assess future risks. Most of the PRINCE2 themes are considered in this process.

In the TS project, the PM confirmed that the objective of the project had been met (Business Case, Plans, and Progress themes) and that staff were ready to move into new teams in TS. The PB agreed to close the project (Organization theme) because its objective had been met and the number of staff devoted to electronic resources tasks had tripled.

In an anonymous survey conducted in October 2016, measures on the effect of the reorganization on job satisfaction were neutral, indicating that job satisfaction overall neither improved nor declined. However, there was considerable variation in individual respondent scores, suggesting that the reorganization improved job satisfaction for some while eroding it for others. One measure of job satisfaction that was clearly achieved was whether staff were working on teams of their choice, with the average response to the statement "I'm on every team that I want to be on" being "mostly agree." However, the four other items measuring job satisfaction achieved only neutral endorsement, leading us to conclude that the objective of improving job satisfaction was not met. We will work in the coming months to identify areas of low job satisfaction and look for ways to address it.

The review of the performance of the project took place with staff in TS (the working groups), the head of Technical Services (the PM), and the head of DDS (the PB). However, this phase of the project remained uncompleted until the fall of 2016 because we did not have a lessons learned log. The lessons learned log is important in PRINCE2 because it allows us to record things that we learned throughout the project to help prevent repetition of mistakes or to help anticipate issues in future projects. This was a missed opportunity to learn from our first experience with PRINCE2, but lessons learned seemed obvious at the time. However, trying to remember these lessons now demonstrates the importance of maintaining the log because it is hard to recall a year later what lessons were learned.

POST-REORGANIZATION STRUCTURE

Two things were made clear to all TS staff from the beginning of this process: we weren't sure that all the changes would work, and, therefore, we would be flexible in our implementation. For example, some of the work put in the domain of a team might look good in theory but end up not being workable in practice, or some staff might find their new responsibilities so unpleasant as to make them miserable, or we might discover after the implementation that the workload isn't balanced properly between the teams. The PMT made clear that if problems arose, everyone in the department would work together to address them.

This approach allowed everyone the freedom to try out things that might make sense without an expectation that it would be a guaranteed success. Nobody would be blamed if things did not work; instead, the issue would be acknowledged, and some other strategy or method would be attempted. This approach received positive feedback from staff and contributed to the reorganization's being a much more positive experience for everyone than it might otherwise have been.

Resolved Issues

The seepage issue noted earlier was one example of things that looked fine on paper but that quickly caused problems when procedures were being drafted and staff began to realize how often a process that was formerly handled by a single person got split up among several staff members on multiple teams. As noted earlier this consequence was sometimes resolved by moving tasks to another team, but in some cases doing so would have essentially stripped a team of a significant percentage of its responsibility. This result in some cases would have required rebalancing the teams or in other cases would have failed to address the skills silo problem that the reorganization was designed to solve.

In the end, seepage was acknowledged, resolved where possible, and monitored where it remained. Now that the one-year anniversary of the reorganization has passed, these problems will be reviewed to learn whether seepage has gone away or needs to be further resolved. We suspect that we will find that we have overcome or ameliorated many of the problems through the course of the year to the point at which the benefits of the reorganization outweigh the costs.

Unresolved Problems

Related to the seepage problem is the difficulty of knowing which team is in the best position to receive new problems, pieces of information, or requests. This uncertainty is partly caused by seepage, which is exemplified when a process moves from one team to another as the process is being addressed. Consequently, selecting the staff member to whom to send a query can depend on the current stage of the process.

Another reason for this problem is that the teams' domains sometimes look arbitrary. For example, collection of use statistics for electronic resources is done after we've acquired a resource and throughout the lifetime of the resource, yet the procedure is carried out by the Electronic Resource Setup team, where one would expect to find only procedures related to the initial acquisition of the resource. Another example involves discerning and documenting which electronic resource content will have perpetual access—a task that one might expect to fall in the domain of licensing and thus lie with the Electronic Resource Setup group but instead is handled by the Subscription Management group. Staff in other parts of the Libraries will not be able to remember these intricacies, so the problem is being addressed by listing the most common responsibilities of each team on the staff Intranet contact page for the department and by prominently including a "Don't know who to contact?" link at the top of the page so that staff can e-mail their questions to a departmental address that will be routed to the appropriate person.

Another unresolved problem is that the responsibilities of the department's two supervisors became muddied by the reorganization. Before the reorganization there were two supervisors—one for Monographs and one for Serials. After the reorganization, there were four teams instead of two, with monographic and serial responsibilities integrated in the four teams and staff serving in any two of the four units. Thus, there is no single supervisor for any of the new teams, and staff reporting lines have not changed, so who reports to which supervisor has become somewhat arbitrary in the new organizational structure.

Although this approach looks very messy and confusing in theory, in practice it has not been a problem. Both supervisors attend all the teams' meetings and are well versed in the activities and issues of all the teams, and although both supervisors have special expertise in the work of the teams that most resemble their former units, they are increasingly familiar with the work of the other teams and are collaborative and cooperative when it comes to making decisions. One supervisor tends to do the scheduling for all the teams but always in consultation with the other supervisor, and there is a little more consultation than previously between the two supervisors about leave requests. A benefit of this approach is that staff within the teams are very engaged in problem solving, something that might not happen if they could easily point to a single person as "responsible" for that team. Although no decisive action has been taken, the past year has demonstrated that a supervisor for each team is not necessarily needed.

LESSONS LEARNED

In the PRINCE2 Closing the Project process, lessons learned are supposed to be documented for future projects in the lessons learned log discussed earlier. Unfortunately, this PRINCE2 tool was ignored, and lessons learned were not documented. However, on reflection, we learned the following.

PRINCE2 was useful, but we would do it better next time.

Some of the PRINCE2 tools were invaluable, especially in the Organization and Plans themes, but we would probably be more flexible and adhere to them more next time. Sometimes we set up plans outside consideration of the framework and then realized later that those plans in fact fit into the PRINCE2 framework. A template and checklists would be useful, and we would create them during the first phase next time. We found that PRINCE2 worked well and made a lot of sense, but it was a different way of thinking about things than we were accustomed to. Documenting the information was very useful, and, at the very least, the business case, plans, and roles should be defined before any project is undertaken. The role of the PB in the managing by exception principle was not followed. Although we did manage by exception, the PB was more involved in the project than was necessary. That involvement was more a matter of personal interest in the department and in the project because using PRINCE2 was an experiment and the PB had the formal training. In future projects, it is expected that the PB will be less involved and will include more than one person.

The PRINCE 2 processes of Starting Up a Project, Directing a Project, and Initiating a Project, when done well, make everything else easy.

Even though we may have struggled with tailoring the project to suit our environment, setting up everything using this method made efforts easy during the project because all those involved knew what they were doing. Once the setup was done, the project rolled along through completion.

Having a mechanism for making changes to the project is essential.

The working groups could and did make suggestions for changes to the project plan where appropriate, as discussed earlier. This component was important because in previous reorganizations in our experience, sometimes specific structures, workflows, or procedures were pushed through even if their benefit was doubted by those implementing or adopting them. There have been various reasons for this result, including lack of clarity about who is allowed to change the plan or reliance on only one person who can change the plan and who is overwhelmed. This project was easy because the plan and stages were in the hands of the staff, new ideas were encouraged, and staff understood what changes they could make and what needed to be referred to a higher ranking staff member. No bottlenecks occurred because a single person had total control or needed to approve all changes. Similarly, all staff members knew their realm of responsibility and worked together because the processes had all been planned for in advance.

Giving staff choices and honoring those choices is key.

Giving staff choices and honoring those choices appeals to human nature. However, if a project's time line is too aggressive, this fact is often neglected in the project planning phase, and people aren't consulted before decisions are made that will affect their work life. Explaining to staff the reason for the changes, providing staff an opportunity to choose what they would like to do in the new structure, then providing staff with a clearly defined role in moving to that new structure set up the project for success from the beginning.

Be ready for staff empowerment.

Although the concept for the project originated with the head of DDS and the head of Technical Services, basically their roles in the project were to manage oversight and exceptions and to make sure that the groups stuck to their plans and schedules. The staff did the work and made most of the decisions; nothing was pushed down from the PM and the PB when the project was initiated. Truthfully, the PM and the PB occasionally had discussions about whether we should "allow" something (a transfer of a task, for example), but we always came back to the question of whether the change affected the business case and was within the tolerances we had set. It is difficult to give up control, but when the staff saw that they had power to make decisions that affected their daily work, they took full advantage and worked to achieve the best outcomes, ultimately completing a successful project.

Sometimes compromise is necessary to achieve all your goals.

The head of Technical Services is still struggling with problems associated with efficiency versus equity and specialization versus generalization. It is more equitable to have balanced workloads for each of the teams, but that approach resulted in more handoffs than was optimal. Specialists who always deal with the more difficult tasks learn to resolve them faster than generalists who only come across the difficult tasks occasionally, but the result is that some crucial skills reside in just two or three staff members. During the project compromises were made, but they will be reexamined to see if they are effectively working out over time.

CONCLUSION

Although the staff in TS are still working through the transition to the new organizational structure, overall the implementation project was successful. Staff members continue to contribute to the success of the department by suggesting changes to workflows or helping to figure out new processes. Given that many library projects are organizational or process-oriented, this project was a good test. The time and energy spent up front in the first phase of the project paid huge dividends in the final phases in which there was little work to do by the PM and the PB, and following the principle of managing by exception made the decision-making process straightforward throughout the project. Overall, the project and the methodology were successful, and PRINCE2 will be used for future projects.

NOTE

1. Andy Murray and Office of Government Commerce, *Managing Successful Projects with PRINCE2*, 5th ed. (London: TSO, 2009).

SIAN BRANNON

7

Triage Succession Planning

How Mass Turnover Required On-the-Spot Mentoring

UPON ARRIVING AT A NEW JOB as manager of a collections depart-ment at a southern research university library, I was faced with imminent turn-over on the team. Four employees had left the organization before I started in my new role and had not been replaced. Among the twenty-six remaining staff (including me), thirteen were eligible to retire, and four were slated to move to another division. Within six months of my arrival, three staff retired. Before the end of my first year, four more retired. And within four years of my arrival, a total of thirteen of the original group had left or been reassigned to other divisions, leaving me with a staff of thirteen. Although it had always been known that people could (and would) leave the organization, little succession planning, cross-training, or documentation of institutional knowledge had been done. This problem required a form of "triage" succession planning to determine the immediate needs of the division in relation to newly set stra-tegic goals of the library that were developed during the year I was hired. In this chapter, I will follow the process of this improvised and ad hoc attempt at succession planning by illustrating the time line I crafted, the meetings that were necessary, and the changes, assessments, mentoring, and planning that took place. In addition, I will reflect on the efficacy of the succession planning and articulate the lessons learned throughout the process.

This research university is located in the southern part of the United States and has over thirty-seven thousand students. The library comprises seven divisions: Public Services (subject librarians, reference, access services, and government documents), Collection Management (technical services, collection development, and preservation), Digital Libraries (user interfaces, systems, and the digital projects lab), External Relations (outreach, communications, and graphic design), Special Collections (archives, music, media, and the remote campus), Facilities and Systems, and Administration. The library has approximately fifty librarians and ninety full-time staff, and our materials budget is approximately $7 million. We have one central library, two branch locations, one additional location on a remote campus, and two remote storage facilities.

I arrived at my library in 2010 from a public library at which I was librarian manager of Technical Services. In 2009 the new dean of Libraries arrived and created the Collection Management Division. The division was made up of three functional areas: Preservation, Collection Development, and Technical Services, all of which reported to me in my new role. The Preservation Department, which consisted of one full-time librarian and two full-time staff members, was responsible for materials processing, bindery operations, and materials repair. This group is located in a remote storage facility one mile from the main campus. The Collection Development Department, with two librarians and one assistant, was officially formed one year before I arrived. Before the department was created, its tasks had been spread across the library, with no formal oversight of the collections budget or evaluation. The three people in the new department were charged with selection, review, gifts, policy development, budget oversight, strategic purchases, accreditation reports, approval plans, and interactions with subject liaison librarians throughout the organization. These obligations proved to be a remarkable amount of work for three people. The Technical Services Department was responsible for general collections cataloging, electronic resources, contracts and licensing, reclassification, ordering, invoicing, and authority control. The staff in the department included a department head, twelve full-time staff, and five librarians, for a total of eighteen staff members. To aid me with supervising these three areas I also had a full-time administrative assistant on my team.

EMERGENCY—TRIAGE NEEDED

On my first day of employment, I learned that retirements were possible for 50 percent of the staff in my division. A further analysis showed that within five years, at least three other division employees would be eligible to retire as well. All staff had institutional knowledge and expertise, and we were in danger of losing essential leadership, knowledge, and skills if all these folks were to leave. In addition, there were other variables affecting our division. These included fluctuations in the materials budget, the library's aspiration to join the Association of Research Libraries (ARL), the transition to implementing the Resource Description and Access (RDA) standard for cataloging, added responsibilities for creating metadata for digital content, and the separation of the team from the main campus because we were housed in the remote storage facility.

After meeting with each staff person individually, I determined that we needed to develop new skills and areas of oversight, especially related to collection management. We lacked statistical analysis abilities, knowledge about grant-seeking and writing proposals, capabilities in computer programming and API (application program interface) creation, and an understanding of the budget procedures of the university. The staff who were left needed to improve their interpersonal communication, visioning, and general "people skills" that enable the division to engage and collaborate with other divisions in the library. Furthermore, staff needed to have emerging technical skills such as non-MARC metadata creation and management, data harvesting, RDA, and integrated library system manipulation.

Most of all, we needed fresh ideas and a willingness to change. Therefore, it was time for a "triage" succession plan. We immediately needed to address current staff capabilities, retirement plans, documentation of responsibilities, and planning for the future.

TIME TO BEGIN

The first thing I did was to create a time line of necessary tasks and objectives. Because I started in December 2010, I developed a set of deadlines for various activities that I had to complete in order to have a succession plan in place by September 2011. In addition, my aim was to provide the staff sufficient time to adjust their "performance agreements" for their annual performance reviews. I outlined the following activities:

- Meet with each of my staff to talk about individual work responsibilities.
- Have first meeting with the department heads to discuss their groups.
- Meet with the departments.
- Have second meeting with department heads to summarize progress; review workflows and document diversity and skill needs.

- Pinpoint key positions of immediate need, finalize desired competencies, and identify potential internal candidates.
- Share progress and plans with dean and associate dean.
- Create development plan for all staff; meet with faculty from library schools in town, discuss succession plan with the university's Equity and Diversity Department, and identify potential mentors.
- Deliver succession plan to the library's dean and associate dean and share the majority of the plan with the Collection Management Division.

When I met with each employee individually, I asked the following six questions:

1. What are your career plans involving this institution?
2. What do you like about working here?
3. Can you boil your job down to five words?
4. What does it take to do your job well?
5. What would you tell someone new in your position?
6. Would you please write down the tasks you complete in a typical day?

Given the time pressure I felt, I was so focused on the impending departures and the lack of documentation of duties and procedures that I aggressively pursued setting up meetings. Because staff were already nervous about a new division head coming in and making a lot of changes, a few of my questions led them to believe that their jobs were in danger. I was slow to catch on, but their responses alerted me to the unfortunate oversight of *not* telling them the purpose of my meeting and what I was trying to accomplish. This was a rookie mistake, yes, and I corrected it by backing off, gathering everyone together, and explaining why I was using my approach. I started with a review of the dean's strategic plan and tried to explain how we fit into the vision. Having been on the job for only a month or so, I found this meeting difficult, but my intent was to get us aligned as a group instead of having the group blindly follow my master plans. Then I explained the concept of succession planning as a true planning exercise with benefits for the future. Following this meeting, staff had a chance to step back and take a look at the division as a whole, and they soon realized that there was definitely a problem. Their long-term loyalty to the institution gave them the motivation to participate, and we began again with the entire team on board. Individual interviews resumed, followed by strategizing meetings with individual department heads concerning their functional areas. A few weeks later I was able to schedule the department meetings.

During the meetings with the department heads, we brainstormed and assessed skills needed for their functional areas, talked about ideal employees, and developed competencies related to their areas. We talked about each employee in their area as individuals, measuring them against desired competencies, and identified probable candidates for future open positions. We then identified potential mentors inside and outside the division that could help foster the desired competencies.

Finally, I advised the department heads that I was considering a reorganization of the division to evenly distribute workloads. For example, one person managed a department of seventeen, while the other two managers had only two employees each. The Technical Services Department head (who was managing the largest group) was relieved by this proposed change, which made for a smoother transition. In the department meetings that followed, I explained where we were in the process, my anticipated time line, and the workflow analysis and documentation of the institutional knowledge that we would develop. The departments agreed to construct rudimentary documentation within three weeks.

DIVERSIFICATION

An apparent need was diversification of the staff. This need seems to be common across libraries, and the lack of diversity was noticeable in the new division. We had a fairly homogeneous department based on such factors as ethnicity, age, skill, and rank and job responsibility of the staff. The division was 88.5 percent Caucasian, 11.5 percent minority, 19 percent male, and 81 percent female. The division was also heavily skewed toward retirees, with an average age of more than fifty, even among the librarians.

The computer skills needed for collection development and technical services functions in libraries were not present among the current staff. Although recent library school graduates were gaining knowledge in and exposure to digital content, metadata, and systems librarianship, the majority of staff in the division were not exposed to this information. Fortunately, most expressed interest in learning! Others went along dutifully. The department heads and I brainstormed about interdivisional activities and skills that would benefit the library as a whole. Then we discussed new "pie-in-the-sky" positions that would be ideal for our team if we could not retrain those already employed.

We noted that we had a plethora of options for cooperating with other divisions in the library in ways not considered before. The Digital Libraries Division needed assistance in metadata creation. Public Services and subject liaisons, focusing more and more on reference and instruction, needed help with collection development, and we certainly could partner with Interlibrary Loan on using their data for selection decisions. The External Relations Division could provide assistance with grants and donors. Collection Management could partner with Administration on materials budget issues and diversification of funding and with Facilities and Systems on enhancing library use statistics and technology.

In Technical Services, the most desirable skills were metadata knowledge, original cataloging experience, and foreign language aptitude. For Collection Development, there was more desperation because it was a smaller department. Needs included having someone knowledgeable about open access materials, ingesting of digital content, and the creation of a data bank for information about collections, use, and other variables for analysis.

Based on the identified skill gaps, we created the following action items in order to delineate the types of employees we needed and the skills they needed to possess:

> Seek qualified candidates who are diverse in gender, race, and age. Obtain summarized demographic information about applicants from the human resources department before interviewing begins to gauge the diversity of the applicant pool.
>
> Seek qualified candidates who may be proficient in multiple languages and have specific training or experiences that will serve our internal and external patrons' needs.
>
> Partner with local library schools and serve as the preferred location for internships. The library may recruit potential employees from this pool.

Through these initial meetings, immediate potential changes came to light. There was a substantiated attitude of adhering to legacy processes and workflows, and there was a lack of newer, more technologically advanced methods for accomplishing tasks. I made decisions to reallocate materials budget funds away from monographs given the change in user needs, and this move changed some staff members' responsibilities. I reorganized the structure of the division to align skill sets and job functions, and I distributed the reporting lines evenly. I decided that the preservation of general collections materials was not as important as the preservation and conservation of rare books and archives, so I collaborated with the assistant dean for Special Collections to transfer the Preservation of Collections Materials Department to Special Collections. Technical Services retained the bindery staff person and operations. Consequently, the full-time administrative assistant for the division left, and we did not fill that open line because Administration repurposed it in another division. Within approximately three months, the division consisted of twenty-three full-time employees, losing one librarian and two staff members.

Despite these changes, we still needed additional tactics to diversify our team. I developed a couple of strategies for doing this, pending retirements. For one thing, there are two library schools near our university. By meeting with the chairs and faculty of the library school departments, I could ascertain whether their curriculum might meet our needs and whether they had their own diversity recruitment strategies as well as make direct contact with potential applicants for future jobs. Another strategy was to speak with the university's Equity and Diversity Department, which is involved in every librarian hire. I needed to understand the department's role in the process and find out what it could do to help me diversify my team. Last, I committed to analyzing each opening as it became available, seeking to partner with other divisions to break down silos and create new, future-focused, striking job descriptions to attract new talent to join our team as well as inspire current employees to strive for new opportunities and develop new skills.

DETERMINING KEY POSITIONS AND POTENTIAL SUCCESSORS

Being brand new in the organization and unfamiliar with the history of the positions or the reasoning behind the current organizational structure of the division, I knew I had to tread lightly in this area. I wanted to determine the key positions that would be needed in a future-thinking and technologically capable division. A combination of factors helped me establish a list of these positions: talks with individuals, current job descriptions, and knowledge of trends in the field.

I made two tables: one identified current key positions (table 7.1), and the other documented the positions that I wanted to create for the future (table 7.2). In the first table, I listed positions that I knew already existed and that I wanted to keep. In the table were a number of considerations. First, we needed to determine the retirement status of the employee currently in the position. Could that employee retire in one to five years or later? Second, we needed to determine how critical the functions of this position are to the division. Some functions are more critical than others and require someone who is ready to contribute to the organization quickly rather than someone who will contribute in six to twelve months. Furthermore, in what order would we fill these positions if they were to become vacant in relatively close succession? Which position presents more loss of organizational knowledge or service interruption? Which would slow things down? Finally, I needed to determine whether I had any internal candidates who could be potential successors for these positions and whether those candidates would be ready in a relatively short time. To assess how critical the position was and to assign priority, I used a scale of 1 to 3, with 1 being the most critical or highest priority. Table 7.1 provides a list of the key positions and a general overview of how one might populate the table. In some instances, there was more than one potential successor.

In table 7.2, I listed the positions that didn't yet exist but that I wanted to create in order to determine if I had any internal candidates who could possibly fill them.

TABLE 7.1

Key existing positions and potential successors

Position Title	Retirement Status of Current Employee	Criticality	Priority	Potential Successor	Ready Now?	Ready in 1–2 Years?
Assistant Dean		1	3	Fergus Elton	No	No
Head of Collection Development	3 years	1	1	Aggie McDuff	No	Yes
				Liam Tennant	No	Yes
Head of Technical Services	3 years	2	1	None—external hire		
Collection Development Librarian	1 year	2	2	Hamish Rye	No	No
Serials Head	3 years	1	1	Fiona Maud	Yes	
Electronic Resources Librarian		2	2	None—external hire		
Cataloging Specialist	1 year	1	1	None—external hire		
Acquisitions Specialist	3 years	3	3	Angus McFew	No	Yes

TABLE 7.2

Desired positions and potential candidates

Position Title	Criticality	Potential Candidate	Ready Now?	Ready in 1–2 Years?
Open Access Collection Librarian	2	None—external hire		
Metadata Specialist	1	Molly McGowan	No	Yes
Collection Analyst Librarian	1	Rhys Mulligan	No	Yes

It should be noted that this step of the succession plan is one for which confidentiality may be necessary. One must not give employees false hopes of promotion nor guarantees of job changes. In addition, some staff may be offended or demoralized if they think that you do not see any future growth for them. Therefore, I worked on this step solely with the department heads and trusted them to be honest in their assessment of their employees and to not divulge the decisions made until we completed the succession planning process and determined the best method to proceed.

IDENTIFYING COMPETENCIES

Following these exercises I felt that I knew our employees and their abilities. We knew the positions that we had, the ones we wanted, and the likelihood that there would be openings. We had some idea of who could be a successor pending a retirement and where we needed to make outside hires due to the lack of qualified internal candidates. It was now time to focus on the general and specific competencies that would be necessary for the key positions.

In general, the department heads and I agreed that "softer skills" had long been overlooked in the division due to the technical nature of cataloging, acquisitions, collection development, and preservation. Instead of focusing on quotas, inputs and outputs, precision of catalog records, and other basic job knowledge, I chose to concentrate on fostering growth in areas such as critical thinking, professionalism, and leadership. This is not to say that other job-related skills were overlooked. We also needed to ensure that the staff were increasing their technological capabilities, commitment to participation in the profession, and understanding of how everyone's duties interacted.

We determined the following to be basic competencies.

Leadership competencies

- Political acumen
- Partnership and tactical alliance development
- Library advocacy
- Strategic planning
- Motivational abilities
- Appreciation for diversity

Management competencies

- Effective time management
- Knowledge of labor-related legal issues (for supervisors)
- Basic budget know-how
- Personnel management and team building
- Policy development and justification

Critical thinking competencies

- Thinking independently, self-starting
- Distinguishing relevant from irrelevant facts
- Reasoning and solving problems
- Knowledge of where to look for information

Communication competencies

- Writing skills, including correct grammar, punctuation, and spelling
- E-mail etiquette
- Public-speaking skills, including giving presentations
- Keeping staff and supervisors informed
- Appropriate body language
- Ability to listen

Professionalism and professional involvement competencies

- Work ethic
- Professional appearance
- Professional ethics
- Dedication to the profession and the division
- Commitment to publishing and presenting (for librarians)

Technology competencies

- Familiarity with desktop PCs; Microsoft Office skills
- Confidence with library automation system
- Working knowledge of electronic resources

Specific position competencies (these vary by position; the following are for the head of collection development)

- Familiarity with the university's degree programs and curriculum
- Knowledge of accreditation requirements
- Relationships with subject liaison librarians
- Supervision of two or more employees
- Outreach capabilities

At this point in the creation of the succession plan, it was time to reconcile identified candidates with key positions by measuring their capabilities within these competencies. This action would allow us to determine how likely it would be for a candidate to be able to transfer into the position and to ascertain areas for needed improvement before opportunities arose.

ASSESSING CANDIDATE COMPETENCY CAPABILITY

I created competency tables for each position, and potential candidates were assigned a score between 1 and 4, indicating their aptitude in each competency. These scores were basically defined as follows:

> 1—Has no skills in this area
>
> 2—Shows basic capabilities; needs development
>
> 3—Very promising; will require occasional guidance and coaching
>
> 4—Excellent capabilities
>
> N/A—not critical for position

To illustrate, we selected Aggie and Liam as potential internal candidates for the position of head of collection development, a position that could become available within three years. This position is high priority, critical to the dean's vision for the library given our goal of joining ARL. I identified this position as one that would need to be filled right away.

Table 7.3 outlines and compares the capabilities of Aggie and Liam across the various competencies and specific job responsibilities. Aggie has talents

TABLE 7.3

Assessing Aggie's and Liam's capability to be head of the Collection Development Department

Head, Collection Development Department	Leadership	Management	Critical Thinking	Business Writing and Communication	Professionalism and Professional Involvement	Technology and Education	Specific Position Skills
Aggie McDuff	2	1	3	2	3	4	4
Liam Tennant	3	2	3	4	4	3	2

*All names are fictional.

in some areas but not others and would require some development. Liam shows more promise, having higher scores in most competencies. With this knowledge, I could decide not only what each candidate would need to do to become a better fit for the position should it come open but also whether the effort would be justified. This process was repeated for every key existing and desired position and took place within just a few days. I made sure to involve the current department heads in evaluating their employees and discussing those employees' scores in each competency. This area is another in which confidentiality is important.

CREATING A PLAN FOR EMPLOYEE DEVELOPMENT

Continuing with the cases of Aggie and Liam and their capabilities related to becoming the head of the Collection Development Department, we see identified areas in which they excel and areas in which they need development. In doing so, the department head, who would soon be retiring, and I documented the skills the internal candidates needed to work on and tried to identify ways in which the candidates could achieve the competencies.

An employee can gain skills through a variety of methods. To gain exposure to leadership theory and critical thinking strategies, the employee can attend online webinars, go to workshops, or research relevant literature. To improve management skills, the employee can be given one or two staff members to supervise and be included in department head meetings. To learn more about business writing and communication, the employee can take university courses offered through the Human Resources Department that would be helpful; specific assignments involving teams and reports can be given to that employee. Similarly, the university's Information Technology (IT) Department offers courses in various desktop applications, and the library's Technology Department and systems librarian can help teach staff about the library's automation system.

A more practical method of imparting skills, especially in the areas of leadership, management, and specific position responsibilities, was to partner the employee with a strong mentor in the area in which I had identified a deficiency. Before moving forward with this step in succession planning, I contacted potential mentors to communicate what I was trying to accomplish and to gauge their interest in being paired with an employee. Most identified mentors worked inside the libraries, but a few did not, especially when it came to gaining the specific position skills that were necessary. The concept of "mentor" was applied loosely and varied from person to person. Some potential successors needed close guidance, while others were more involved in job-shadowing.

For the position of head of the Collection Development Department, we first considered Aggie. After assessing her capabilities in the various competencies, we determined that she was good at the technological skills required for the position and good at specific job responsibilities, but she lacked management skills and experience and was marginally proficient in leadership and critical thinking. After conversations with the department head, I made Aggie a team supervisor of acquisitions and selection in the Collection Development Department. Although the head of the department would still be responsible for "signing time cards," so to speak, Aggie would be responsible for monitoring time, overseeing the projects of the team, and meeting deadlines. These tasks would give her experience with management. To convey leadership and critical thinking skills, I identified a potential mentor for Aggie in another division. This mentor had worked for the libraries for many years and was respected as a transformative person who had led a department through a difficult change. Knowing that the situation had required researching of options and tough decision making, I believed that this individual would be able to assist Aggie in improving her leadership and critical thinking skills.

We applied the same process to Liam. He had relatively good scores across the board, but he scored lowest in the job responsibilities specific to the position of head of Collection Development. To remedy this lack, I found multiple webinars and information resources for Liam to review and report on. Like Aggie, Liam had insufficient management skills, and the development solution was the same—making him a team leader over a specific project. I also determined that Liam could participate in various committees on campus to gain exposure to more curriculum issues and could visit with subject liaisons and attend faculty meetings to build relationships. To this end, I identified a mentor for Liam from Reference who had extensive subject liaison responsibilities.

Though the department head and I brainstormed methods to help the employees gain needed skills, and though we identified potential mentors, we needed to bring in the employees at this point to gauge their interest in the path we were planning. Delivering this information is a delicate task. I wanted to convey that I saw promise in each employee and wanted to help the individuals develop, but I needed to communicate that message in a way that offered no guarantees. Most employees were amenable and eager to further their careers. Even though I had met with every employee when I first arrived and tried to identify potential successors that I believed to be interested in the key positions, it turned out that some employees changed their minds. Aggie decided that she wanted to go back to school and did not want to move up in the organization at that time. Liam, however, was extremely fascinated with the opportunity to develop his skills. He went above and beyond what we prescribed.

Creating development plans for internal candidates is relatively simple: identify gaps, find methods to gain new skills, locate a potential mentor, talk to the employee, set goals, and make a time line. When it came to those positions for which there were no viable internal candidates, the development plan transformed into more of a "search" plan whereby we had to survey the field, craft new job descriptions, make a detailed strategy for conducting searches, ask the potential retirees for recommendations, and network through conferences, workshops, and electronic discussion lists, hoping to find ideal candidates.

COMMUNICATING AND REFLECTING

After I created development plans and search strategies, I presented a full succession planning document to the dean for his consideration. Although he knew that many of the employees in the Collection Management Division had worked for the libraries for a long time, he was unaware of how drastic the pending retirement situation was. Therefore, the succession plan provided me with some leverage in preparing him for moving the division into modern times with new skill sets. The plan also allowed me to demonstrate the anemic state of the Collection Development Department compared to its responsibilities, which provided for support in keeping positions when staff retired (and even helped me add a new one!).

Then it came time to discuss the plan with the division staff. Because we had already experienced the Preservation Department's departure, two retirements, and the loss of the administrative assistant position, the staff were even more aware that complacency was misguided and that the need for documentation, review, and training was more important than ever. I needed to be careful about how I presented information. For example, Aggie and Liam did not need to know how the other scored in competency capabilities for the key position. Also, staff didn't need to be afraid that their positions might not be considered key. Instead, I talked in broad terms about the future, about wanting to gain skills, and about fostering development within the library.

This process took approximately five months. This amount of time is less than optimal for truly examining one's staff without knowledge of the relevant workloads, potential changes in workflows, or even the true culture of the workplace. However, given the swift departure of a number of eligible-for-retirement staff, and given how slow the hiring process can be in academic libraries (especially for librarians . . .), it behooved me to rapidly support internal growth and maintenance of institutional knowledge.

Incorporating true mentorship into the triage succession plan effort was difficult. Being new at the institution, I was heavily reliant on my department heads to judge whom to approach to be mentors. In fact, the true "mentoring" could not occur until after the plan was completed. Learning people's strengths and areas of concern over a longer period means better mentor/mentee matches can be made.

In the few years since the plan was created, nine of the eligible employees have retired. The plan became more fluid, and as we filled positions from the outside, we put those candidates through the same scrutiny. We have created new positions and reviewed them annually to determine whether they are key. We have promoted two librarians to higher positions and changed one staff line to a librarian line, thus developing through training and mentorship three people we had identified as internal candidates (including Liam!).

A few major lessons stood out in conducting the succession planning process in five months:

- Tell people what's going on before you start.
- Make sure that you can control how, when, and to whom certain information is communicated. Parts of the plan should not be shared outside management.
- Involve potential mentors as early as possible in the process.
- Make sure that staff are aware that promotion is not guaranteed. Ultimately, the decision is up to the dean.
- Last, but most important, your workflows, your technology, and your needs will change. Staff come and go. Even if you think you have "closed the loop," and no matter how fast you do it, succession planning is never really *over*. It may have less urgency, but it will never have less importance.

MAURITA BALDOCK and
VERÓNICA REYES-ESCUDERO

8

The Archivist Apprenticeship

Partnering with the Knowledge River Program Diversity Initiative

THE UNIVERSITY OF ARIZONA LIBRARIES (UAL) is committed to initiatives that promote diversity and inclusion within its staff, faculty, and collections as well as to its service to students, faculty, and the community. Among the many strategies is the University of Arizona Libraries Special Collections (UALSC) partnership with the Knowledge River (KR) program on campus. This program is one of the few successful initiatives in the country that works to increase the number of librarians from and interested in serving underrepresented groups. Our partnership with this program has proven to be a success, but it initially required a challenging amount of dedication and commitment from the librarians and archivists as well as collaboration with the program leaders. This case study focuses on UALSC's partnership with KR and its development into a successful program for both the institution and the students.

BACKGROUND

The Knowledge River program began in 2002 at the School of Information Resources and Library Science (SIRLS), now known as the iSchool, at the University of Arizona. The program specializes in educating information professionals who have "experience with and are committed to the information needs of Latino and Native American populations." The program reflects a wide view of diversity, equity, and inclusion but focuses on Latino and Native American communities because they reflect the diverse and often underserved populations in Arizona and the Southwest. The program also seeks to foster an understanding of library challenges specifically from Latino and Native American perspectives and "advocates for culturally sensitive library and information services to these communities" (https://ischool.arizona.edu/knowledge-river-0). Students in the iSchool take courses in the program that are relevant to the goals of KR, such as an introductory course entitled "Information Environments from Library and Hispanic and Native American Perspectives." Largely funded by a grant from the Institute of Museum and Library Services (IMLS) with support from the UAL and other cultural institutions in the Tucson area, the KR program was one of the first to address diversity in library and information science education. Students who are accepted to the Knowledge River program receive tuition remission using IMLS funds and are provided placements as graduate assistants (GAs) at partnering institutions.

In Special Collections, the GA salaries and employee-related expenses are committed from UAL funds specifically for GAs. One funder is the Udall Foundation, a federal agency that funds programs that support the legacy of Arizona politicians Stewart L. Udall and Morris K. Udall.[1] Because UALSC is the custodian of the papers of these two politicians, we receive funding for graduate students to work on political collections or collections related to the environment or to Native American issues, which were main interests of the Udalls. Other funding for students is provided by an endowment created from the generosity of Katheryne B. Willock, a private donor who supports the work of the library and its students. These funds can be used for any GAs, but Special Collections has committed to specifically having KR students fill the positions.

In addition to graduate assistantships that provide real-world practicums, the KR program provides a cohort experience in which students take classes and participate in activities together. This experience is one of the many advantages of the program because most of the classes in the iSchool are now online with little face-to-face student interaction. The partnering institutions are crucial to the mission of the program because they provide practical work experience for the students and general guidance in the profession. Additional partners in the program have included other libraries and museums on the University of Arizona's campus, such as the Arizona Health Sciences Library and the Arizona State Museum, as well as other local and state libraries, such as the Pima County Public Library and the Arizona State Library. The program has been very successful throughout its history in receiving multiple IMLS grants and has trained more than 170 scholars and librarians. Graduates of the KR program are working as library and information professionals all over the country.

The library faculty and archivists in UALSC are pleased to be a partner in the program and to be contributing to our libraries' and professional organizations' diversity goals. Special Collections is a natural fit for the KR program because our rare books and manuscript collections include materials relating to the history of Arizona and the Southwest. Many of these collections relate to Native American tribes in the Southwest and focus on political and humanitarian issues as well as everyday life in the Arizona and Mexico Borderlands region. The objective for our participation in the program is to attract underrepresented students into the archival and special collections field in order to increase diversity in the profession. We accomplish this goal by providing foundational experience in archival work, enhancing access to collections of underrepresented populations, and providing real-world experience in developing culturally competent individuals.

Diversity in the library and archive profession is a common challenge for many library and information science programs and professional organizations. The Association of Research Libraries (ARL) has been a leader in supporting programs that work toward diversifying the profession, such as the Initiative to Recruit a Diverse Workforce, the Leadership and Career Development Program, the ARL/Society of American Archivists (SAA) Mosaic Program, and the ARL Career Enhancement Program. Other professional organizations such as the Association of College and Research Libraries' Rare Books and Manuscripts Section (RBMS) and SAA also have included diversity charges and statements for their membership. RBMS clearly states its charge:

> To encourage members of underrepresented racial and ethnic groups to join and participate in RBMS; to recruit members of these groups into the Special Collections profession; to partner with other groups in the library field that focus on diversity or diverse collections; to generate and facilitate seminars, workshops, and programs about collecting materials related to racial and ethnic groups and providing outreach to patrons from diverse racial and ethnic backgrounds. (http://rbms.info/diversity/)

Similarly, the SAA Statement on Diversity and Inclusion begins,

> As a professional association that benefits from the participation of people from all backgrounds, the Society of American Archivists strives to ensure that its membership, the holdings that archivists

acquire and manage, and the users whom archivists serve reflect the evolving diversity of society. (http://www2.archivists.org/statements/saa-statement-on-diversity-and-inclusion)

It only follows that as professionals in the field and members of these organizations, we would feel compelled to help in the attainment of these goals.

GROWING PAINS

From its beginning, the KR program was well crafted and its goals admirable. However, as with any new initiative, the initial partnership between the program and Special Collections had its share of issues and complications. Generally speaking, and from the perspective of the library faculty who would serve as supervisors, lines of communication were not well defined, and the goals of the program were not clearly shared with library faculty who would serve as supervisors. Library faculty were not brought into discussions early on so as to develop clear understanding of the goals or logistics of the program. For instance, GA placements were generally chosen by the KR manager and a library administrative staff member appointed to handle placements without consulting with the supervisors or faculty members at partnering departments within UA Libraries. This approach sometimes meant that supervisors in Special Collections had little understanding of the experience of the GAs and why they were placed in Special Collections. At times the GAs were not an appropriate fit for Special Collections. Sometimes these placements would be for an entire school year or sometimes for just one semester, which made it more difficult to plan projects.

During the first three to four years of our partnership with the KR program, Special Collections had limited staff and was without a full-time director. Often, the students joining Special Collections were just beginning library school, had limited job experience, and had not yet had the opportunity to learn much about libraries, much less about archives. Similar to the general public, many of these students did not really understand how archives work or what archivists do. This lack of understanding meant that a significant time commitment by the supervisors was needed to appropriately train the students. With the UA experiencing growing pains caused by reorganization and the loss of staff and state funding, the graduate assistantships in the early to mid-2000s were treated solely as a job. Unfortunately, once a GA was hired, there was little Special Collections could do beyond supplying basic supervision for reference work and providing a foundation in arrangement and description with a few additional discreet projects. Often the students' work included just-in-time needs of the department, such as pulling and shelving materials for class instruction, answering reference requests, and assisting with bibliographic holding checks. Supervisors would manage the GAs, but mentoring and coaching of students were not initially part of the Special Collections program. Hence, in these first few years, two major issues threatened to undermine the success of the program—first, the lack of a programmatic approach to the GAs, and second, the limited amount of staff and time library faculty could devote to the students.

Nonetheless, the librarians and archival faculty as well as the institution were committed to continuing the partnership due to the library administration's commitment to diversity within the library and the profession. By the mid-2000s Special Collections had hired two additional archivists, which increased the department to four professional staff; however, Special Collections still did not have a permanent director. With a processing archivist in place, the GAs were now assigned to her because she managed the fund for the GA salaries. This arrangement meant that the program was generally working better because the students were receiving a quality experience with training in archival arrangement and description. However, we still did not have onboarding plans, training plans, or long-term, well-designed project assignments for the students. This lack of programming was problematic because students were not always clear about workplace expectations and would often miss work without communicating the absences to their supervisors. Without a director and with limited librarian and archivist faculty, supervisors were tasked with multiple responsibilities and were not able to provide more than basic supervision. Although supervisors wanted to provide some mentorship, any mentoring was generally informal. These problems necessitated a reassessment of how things were working and a decision regarding our considerable institutional commitment at many levels.

MOVING FORWARD

The 2010 Knowledge River grant cycle brought about an opportunity that served as an impetus for Special Collections to refocus the work with KR graduate assistants. The KR program manager at the iSchool who was writing the grant for the continuation of the KR program called on the main supervisors in Special Collections to review the grant in order to obtain additional funding from IMLS. This review also became an opportunity for GA supervisors in the partner institutions to meet each other to brainstorm ideas for improving the program at our respective institutions because most of the partnering institutions were accustomed to acting independently of each other. It was in the writing of the grant proposal that we were finally able to collaborate to understand the expected outcomes that had not always been clear to us. Because the supervisors were involved and because we worked directly with the program manager, the deliverables seemed more feasible, and we became even more committed to continuing the program with improvements. We set out to refocus our approach and to include mentoring and coaching along with some changes in how we worked with the GAs.

And though the commitment to the program had wavered during the mid-2000s, this direct collaboration reinvigorated our commitment, and our internal program flourished. With better communication, a clearer understanding of the objectives of the KR program, better staffing within Special Collections, and the commitment of library leadership to the program, we were able to make the program better for the librarians, the UA Libraries, Special Collections, and the student GAs. Working with supervisors and the KR program manager, we carefully matched students with our department. We also took placement a step farther by requiring an interview not only to ensure a good fit but also to provide students with experience in interviewing and to demonstrate that the graduate assistantship was indeed a job. This process has been helpful because we often discover students who have specific skills, such as Spanish-language skills, that will be useful for our projects. We shifted from just-in-time assignments to project-based assignments, established clear lines of reporting and supervision, and created a faculty contact charged with mentoring, coaching, and articulating workplace expectations during the onboarding process.

We also developed a more comprehensive program that included training in the fundamentals of arrangement and description. The training demonstrated to the GAs how to effectively process archival materials. This archival processing training included having the GAs read published articles and manuals on the topic and discuss ideas with their supervisor. While they are working through the intellectual challenges, they begin by processing a small collection before they move on to larger collections. The supervisor now guides them on the survey, rehousing, arrangement, and description necessary for the collection. Internal processing guides were created at this time to facilitate learning. Once the collection is processed, the students write a finding aid for the archival collection and are taught how to put the finding aid online and make it searchable through Encoded Archival Description (EAD). Generally, this initial process takes one to two months of the students' time and assures us that the students understand archival processing. The finding aid that they have prepared can be used as an example of their work when they apply for internships or jobs. The training is now standardized, and the learning objectives apply to all new graduate assistants, which prepares them for more advanced processing and EAD creation tasks.

Once trained in archival processing, the GAs work with their supervisor who takes them through their project-based assignments. These assignments now include more advanced projects, such as archival research assistance, display and exhibition development, digital collections development, and additional archival collections processing. Two examples of student involvement are the digital exhibitions *La Vida Fronteriza: Church, Economy and Daily*

Life—Excerpts from the De la Torre Family Papers and *The Documented Border: An Open Access Digital Archive.* For *La Vida Fronteriza,* the students cocurated, researched, and designed the exhibition and provided full contextual annotations in English and Spanish for the initial items selected (see http:// speccoll.library.arizona.edu/online-exhibits/exhibits/show/delatorre/intro). For *The Documented Border,* the KR student listened to audio interviews and provided summaries in English and Spanish along with descriptive metadata (see http://speccoll.library.arizona.edu/online-exhibits/exhibits/show/docu mented-border/intro). Other KR students have assisted with physical displays or exhibitions, learning the process of curation, archival research, writing of annotations, handling of material, and exhibition installation. Another KR project included a redesign of an exhibition space devoted to our congressional papers. The student selected ephemera and images from nine congressional collections and prepared materials and labels for cases and a wall display that have received many compliments from patrons as well as members of the library administration. These long-term assignments are examples of the explicit learning outcomes that are now outlined in the KR program.

In a 2010 KR survey, students and alumni recommended more mentorship opportunities, and Special Collections, with more time and staffing, was able to respond. We now have a formalized mentorship program that assists the GAs in becoming professionals in the field. Special Collections mentors have ongoing, biweekly meetings with the students to set and review work expectations. Coaching related to workplace and professional behaviors is an important aspect of the program and often occurs during these meetings. The biweekly meetings also serve as a place to safely discuss concerns or issues that students are having and to advise students about how to resolve those issues. In these meetings, the mentors encourage the GAs to discuss what they are learning in the classroom and to compare this knowledge to their experience in Special Collections. The archivists and librarians also provide mentorship in broader ways, such as providing the students with guidance about the library and archival fields and advising them about how to become involved in various local, regional, or national groups. We encourage the GAs to present papers or posters at conferences, and many have presented on their work in Special Collections at the annual Arizona Archives Summit as well as other national conferences. We often take the GAs to visit with potential collection donors to help the students better understand the importance and sensitivity of donor relations and cultural competence. Because UA's iSchool is largely an online program, many of the GAs coming to work in Special Collections do not physically meet with their professors or with many fellow students; thus, we often serve as a main source for suggestions, encouragement, and references for potential internships and jobs.

Along with the mentorship, the KR graduate assistants are required to complete duties beyond those of other student workers. One such task was to complete a weekly posting about their projects, learning, and accomplishments on the blog *Archivist Apprenticeship* (https://archivistapprenticeship.wordpress.com/). The students take turns completing the weekly posts. We provide them guidance on potential topics but allow the students the freedom to discuss what they are working on and what they find interesting about their projects. These posts are a space for students to describe some of their favorite items in the collections and what they enjoy about their projects in a more personal manner. The posts also serve as a way for funders of the KR program and donors of materials to see their projects and to better understand the benefits and impact of the program. One donor of material learned through a blog post that a student was working on his collection and contacted us to express how pleased he was to read that the materials were being organized and would be made available.

At the end of their last semester, KR students are expected to give a capstone presentation showcasing their accomplishments. The presentation takes place in Special Collections and is open to library staff and faculty as well as funders, peers, and iSchool faculty. This showcase also allows the students to demonstrate their personal and professional growth and gain experience in public speaking. A representative from the Udall Foundation regularly attends these presentations and has asked Udall-funded students to contribute their stories to the "Legacy Stories" section of the Udall Foundation website. These capstone presentations evolved into student video interviews that were shared with others, producing positive results. The KR manager shares these videos with prospective KR students to demonstrate the projects that KR students are expected to accomplish. One student specifically asked to be placed in Special Collections after watching videos of past students describing their projects.

CHALLENGES AND LESSONS LEARNED

The training and mentoring that we provide to the KR students are stimulating but also challenging for the librarians and archivists. Because of our institutional commitment to student engagement and diversity, we worked through the challenges. In addition, it is clear that the benefits as articulated in the program's goals far outweigh the challenges. With more staff and more training materials prepared and available, we are better able to devote our time while ensuring that the GAs are properly trained. We have also learned to manage our expectations about what students can do, and we often invest heavily in preparing them to be able to independently complete complex projects.

With the improvements we have made over the years in partnership with the KR program, we have seen the impact the program has on our GAs. The regular meetings with their supervisor or mentor help ensure that the students work on schedule and help us identify problems early. In addition, a Special Collections administrative assistant tracks the students' time. We now work with the KR program manager to accept only students who can be placed in Special Collections for an entire school year. We learned that training students in archival work often takes almost an entire semester, so it is more efficient and fruitful to have the students work a second semester with us so that they can accomplish projects on their own. Setting expectations for the students at the beginning of the assistantship has eliminated confusion because they understand the high expectations that are required for the work. As a result of interviewing potential candidates to ensure better placements and ensuring that all students have a strong foundation in archival processing, we have seen students successfully complete their graduate assistantships and demonstrate projects to potential employers. The Special Collections faculty have also seen an improvement in the quality of GA work, engagement, and commitment with no absenteeism.

CONCLUSION

Our time commitment to the program has proven to be beneficial to Special Collections and to the KR graduate assistants. Although efforts such as ARL's suite of diversity programs and the KR program have helped increase the number of underrepresented individuals in the profession, those numbers are still not representative of the growing diverse population of the United States. More needs to be done, and institutional commitment is crucial in these endeavors. Because the KR program focuses on educating information professionals who have an interest in serving Latino or Native American communities, many students are often from these backgrounds. For many, this is the first time they have worked with archival material, and the collections give them a sense of how their communities are represented in the archival record. As a result, they benefit from working with our Native American and Borderlands archival collections.

Some of our library faculty members are of Latino and Native American backgrounds and are able to serve as guides to the library and archives fields. One student remarked that our library is unusual in its diversity in staff and faculty compared with other places she had interned.

Our partnership with the KR program exposes many students to archives who may not have initially considered this career path. We believe that our efforts in training and mentoring students promote diversity within the library and archives professions. The KR program in general has proven to be successful in encouraging students to enter the iSchool and complete their graduate studies. The graduation rate for KR students in the iSchool is 95 percent. Many KR students who have worked as graduate assistants in UALSC now hold successful positions in the field. Since 2004, fourteen out of twenty-one UALSC Knowledge River graduate assistants have become established in the special collections and archival field or are pursuing higher degrees, and six have established themselves in other fields of librarianship.[2]

The KR students' backgrounds and skills are also beneficial to our own strategic initiatives. We have had students with strong Spanish-language skills work on projects such as processing collections with largely Spanish-language materials or providing Spanish and English bilingual summaries of interviews with journalists working in dangerous areas near the border with Mexico. Other students have assisted with research for exhibitions requiring exceptional command of the Spanish language and with the creation of bilingual labels and metadata for exhibitions or digital collections. Other projects have included piloting translations of finding aids into Spanish and selecting photos from our Arizona, Southwestern, and Borderlands collections for digitization as well as providing descriptive metadata for them. Educating KR students, who are often very involved in their communities, about our collections has helped us reach out and has opened doors for us to work with local Native American tribes regarding tribal materials that we have in our collection.

Our fifteen-year partnership with the KR program may have initially been unclear in expectations and commitments. However, we have worked to solve these problems creatively through more sufficient staffing and planning as well as better communication with students and the program manager. With clear expectations, training, mentoring, coaching, and more project-based assignments, our students now leave with tangible evidence of their accomplishments for future employers as well as professional savvy and polish. We recognize that the sustainability of the program is fragile because the KR program relies on grant funding and because our students' wages and employee-related expenses are paid by outside donors. However, we believe that our efforts to document the work of the students and the success of the program, such as through the student blog and videos, will aid us in continuing to find financial support. Our participation in the program to train a diverse cross section of librarians for the future demonstrates how the UALSC values diversity. We not only have realized our objective of attracting students from underrepresented communities to our profession but also have sent forth many capable professionals to become agents of change.

NOTES

1. For more information on scholarships and programs funded by the Udall Foundation, see http://udall.gov/.
2. Before 2004, we did not keep track of KR students after graduation.

9

One Incident of Violence, or, It Will Never Be the Same

AS SOON AS I WALKED IN THE MAIN DOOR I saw the blood on the floor; you could see it trailing down the stairs, across the foyer, and into the covered pedway between buildings. Campus Security was on scene, and staff were milling about through the turnstiles and back into the service area. My first question to the officer who stepped forward was "Is the building secure?" Hearing an affirmative, I turned to the staff and moved with them into the office area. Everyone was trying to talk at once, asking what had happened and who had been injured. My voice trembled as I said, "I don't know, but the building has been secured. Remain in the office area, and I will be back as soon as I can." With the front stairwell now festooned with yellow crime tape and signs advising that the stairway wasn't in use, I turned toward the staff elevator at the back of the floor, reminding myself to walk and not to break into a run.

My title is assistant dean for Administration. Although I had faced many situations that seemed critical at the time, one violent incident was enough to convince me that nothing is more important than the safety and security of the library and campus community.

THE ORGANIZATIONAL CONTEXT

The University of the Prairies is a century-old, public university that falls into the research doctoral classification in the Carnegie Classification of Institutions of Higher Education. More than fifty-nine thousand students, thirteen thousand faculty, and ten thousand staff constitute a vibrant research and learning community. The library is one of the largest ARL libraries in the country and is organized along hierarchical lines with six subject libraries reporting to the dean through heads of libraries. The dean, assistant deans, and heads of libraries compose the Administration Team and take responsibility for the overall management of the library. The Taylor Library is the site of the incident just described. It occurred on a beautiful spring afternoon near the beginning of March. With Reading Week over and final exams scheduled for the first two weeks of April, the libraries were full of students studying and working on term papers.

There had never been a violent incident in any of the campus libraries. It was even fairly uncommon for Campus Security to be called to deal with nonviolent incidents such as panhandling at the entrance or thefts of backpacks and books. Although staff were urged to be watchful and immediately report any irregular incidents, most staff would have agreed that the library was a safe and secure environment in which to work.

CAST OF CHARACTERS

Various members of library and administrative staff play a part in the case described in this chapter, along with concerned students and observers. Principal characters include the following:

- A student
- His three attackers
- Mary Rodriguez, circulation staff member, the Taylor Library
- Arlene Flaherty, circulation staff member
- Dean of Libraries
- Assistant dean for Administration
- Head of the Taylor Library
- Dr. Ford, wellness counselor
- Al Jensen, Campus Security
- Other members of circulation staff at various campus libraries

THE CASE

The case consists of a violent attack and its aftermath, including the reactions of library staff and others who assembled to deal with the consequences. Relevant data have been provided in order to introduce a dilemma, questions for discussion, and key learning points.

The Attack

Three young men walked up to the third floor of the Taylor Library and spread out, walking along the perimeters of the floor where the study carrels were located. A few students looked up as the young men went by, but no one was unduly alarmed by their presence. The three didn't carry books or backpacks, but they looked enough like the other students that no one found anything remarkable; in fact, few students could later describe what the men looked like or how many of them there were. It was the rush toward a particular carrel and a sharp cry of pain that raised heads. It was described later as a flurry of blows and cries. It looked as though someone was being beaten; no one ever saw a weapon. By the time the students around the carrel where the attack occurred were on their feet, the young men were gone. The carrel's occupant rose to his feet, hunched, his hands clasped over his stomach, and started to run for the stairs. A few students called out, started toward him, but he ignored them all and continued out into the stairwell and down the stairs. As he ran, the students near enough could see blood leaking through his fingers to splash on the floor behind him. He ran out of the library and across the quad to the University Health Center. Apparently he fell several times but got to his feet and ran on. When he arrived at University Health, staff provided emergency care, called an ambulance, and took him to the University Hospital three blocks away. He was in surgery less than an hour later.

The Aftermath

Mary Rodriguez and Arlene Flaherty were on duty at the circulation desk near the bottom of the stairs in the Taylor Library. They both heard feet running down the stairs, but only Mary saw the young man with his hands to his stomach who ran through the turnstiles and headed toward the University Health Center. She was still looking after him when a second student came leaping down the stairs and rushed up to Mary and Arlene. "Call the police," he yelled, "someone has been stabbed!" Arlene got to the phone first and called Campus Security. Meanwhile other students had fled down the stairs, avoiding the splashes of blood as they came, and had gathered around the circulation desk.

Members of the circulation staff assured them that Campus Security had been called and that as far as they knew the building was safe and to please remain in the circulation area. One of the staff called Library Administration and the dean arrived in the circulation area as Campus Security did. The crowd of students and staff in the circulation area was asked to remain there while the building was secured. Members of Campus Security and new arrivals from the city police service went floor to floor asking students to leave the building for the rest of the day. Students still on the floor where the attack had occurred were brought down and detained no further if they had not witnessed the incident. Mary and Arlene and three student witnesses were taken to the dean's office. The rest of the staff members were milling around in the service area; no one had seen what had happened, no one was sure exactly what had happened. Two officers stood at each of the stairwells and elevators as the building was being vacated.

When I arrived on the scene, I was staggered by what I could see and by the various versions of the event that I heard. After I spoke to the circulation staff and assured them that I would be back, it took everything I had not to run to the staff elevator. In Library Administration I spoke briefly to the dean, sent a message to the other campus libraries advising them of the incident, then returned to the main floor along with the head of the Taylor Library who had just returned from a meeting. Some of the staff had questions and seemed to want to talk about what had happened, but there wasn't much to know; others were very silent. I was able to tell the staff that the building had been fully searched and declared secure and that the injured student had received emergency care. Staff were advised that if they felt they needed to talk to someone, they could contact University Wellness where they would be directed to a counselor. I also advised that the building would remain open, but staff were allowed to go home if they wished. Although some staff members were glad to go home, others opted to work quietly in the office till their rides were available. When I finally left the building at the end of the day, cleaning staff were at work cleaning the floor of the blood that had marked the trail of the injured student. For some reason, that act meant a lot to me. It seemed to signal a normalcy that we actually weren't going to feel for some time.

The Next Day

The next day the floor was clean again, the yellow tape removed from the stairwell, and the head of the Taylor Library and I met with the circulation staff to update them about what we now knew, which was very little, and to ask how staff members were feeling. A few staff members reported a sleepless night, and many expressed concern about the student who had been attacked. Mary and Arlene were among the staff who were silent. They had been interviewed by Campus Security and the city police service the day before but had little to tell.

I reminded staff that the university's Wellness Plan provider was making counselors available to us and that students could also be directed to those services. Individuals were encouraged to call and talk to a counselor as they wished, but we had also arranged for a counselor, Dr. Ford, to talk to all staff who had been in the Taylor Library when the incident occurred. Al Jensen from Campus Security had also offered to talk to us as a group. The group meeting was not mandatory, but I encouraged everyone to attend.

The room was full of staff when Dr. Ford and Al Jensen entered. Dr. Ford did a good job of explaining the emotional and psychological response to violence, and staff listened, but there were few questions. When Al stepped to the front of the room, hands immediately shot into the air. Staff had many questions for him, ranging from why this student and this library to the risk of it happening again to the protocol and response time of Campus Security in the event of a future incident. Al calmly answered all the questions, assuring staff that this was not a random act, that the attackers were known to the student, and that it was a targeted and gang-related incident. The student just happened to be on campus when his attackers found him, and the risks were very low of it ever happening again. Although staff listened politely, the questions turned to the safety of staff working in the evenings—could they be issued panic buttons? Would Campus Security do regular patrols? What were the risks of working alone in the evenings? Although Al answered the questions as best he could, assuring staff that this was an isolated incident and that by and large the campus and the libraries were safe places to work, staff didn't seem to be in a mood to be reassured. The meeting didn't end on a bad note; it just felt a bit sour and resentful.

It Will Never Be the Same

Spring and summer hours are always reviewed in mid-March, and decisions are made about casual staffing budgets for the spring and summer months. These discussions are usually straightforward, but not this time. Evening shifts in spring and summer are never popular, but everyone takes a turn. This year was different. Supervisors in almost all the libraries started reporting that staff were reluctant to work evenings. The smaller libraries usually have just one staff member on duty. This was a particular problem—no one wanted to be on duty alone. In fact, no one wanted to work evenings. I went to the various libraries along with a member of Campus Security and met with the staff. We went over the security policy and protocols as well as the various measures that staff could initiate if they became concerned and felt that their safety was threatened for any reason. Our presentation was rational and reasoned, and with few exceptions it seemed to fall on deaf ears. Staff were obviously resentful. For some reason it didn't even seem to be the Taylor Library staff who were most affected. It was staff in the other libraries who wouldn't be placated. How did I know that another attack wouldn't happen? What if someone came in with a gun next time? What if someone crept up behind them with a knife? The what-ifs were endless, and no response I could make was good enough.

The Dilemma

Extended hours, including evenings and weekends, are a fact of life in large academic libraries, and the University of the Prairies Library is no exception. Although some casual staff are employed, permanent members of staff are scheduled to provide service during hours of opening. Some staff, particularly in the smaller libraries, can be alone at service desks for periods of time. The library doesn't have the staffing resources to double-shift or to hire casual staff just to "be with" regular staff at service desks. Staff and supervisors are trained in emergency protocols and procedures, but it is also the nature of emergency situations that not every eventuality can be accounted for or controlled. Staff understand the security policy, who to phone, when Campus Security will come by, that they will be accompanied to their vehicles after work if they wish. But all these things depend on staff members having a sense that they are safe and secure in the workplace. When that feeling disappears, there is no rationale or policy that will fill the void.

QUESTIONS FOR DISCUSSION

Incidents such as the one described in this case are not unusual in large academic libraries. Discussion questions such as the following should encourage you to think about the case from the perspective of a manager or leader who has the responsibility to ensure that the library is a safe and secure space for staff and for all members of the university community.

> Does your organization have security safeguards in place? Is every employee aware of these safeguards?
>
> What emergency response and notification training does your organization provide to all your employees?
>
> Do you require additional emergency response training for your supervisory and management staff?
>
> How does your security department respond when employees are involved in an incident of violence and emergency?
>
> How effective is your human resources department in dealing with issues of employee safety and involvement in violent incidents and have human resources staff received the most updated training?

KEY LEARNING POINTS

Organizations often think in terms of crisis management or business continuity planning, and this preparation is critically important. However, although issues of safety, security, and risk management demand that organizations answer the questions just outlined, there are other issues that planning and preparation can't foresee and that come to the fore in the event of a violent incident or even natural or environmental disasters.

Lessons can be learned from crisis situations: systems fail, the picture is distorted and it is difficult to acquire the big picture of the crisis, time is compressed, authority is limited and limiting, new leadership often emerges.[1] These lessons are illustrated in the Taylor Library stabbing incident. The usual systems that would have been used to alert staff and students in an emergency situation (a loudspeaker, for example) weren't used because of the panic that might ensue among the occupants (later estimated at 600 to 750 students and staff members) of a six-floor building with one of two stairwells blocked off and one set of public elevators in operation. Security personnel went floor to floor to speak to occupants directly and evacuate the floors. Once that was done, any reassurances seemed hollow until there was a sense of why the attack had occurred and knowledge that the student had survived it. The few direct witnesses to the incident were finally identified and statements taken from them, but stories and rumors were rampant, and it was very difficult to know exactly what had happened. The compression of time was very evident and affected the ability to respond; it became clear that trying to bring events under control only heightened the sense of the urgency of the moment. Informing the other libraries and other staff as well as university administration simply led to more questions for which there were no answers and served to escalate the scope of the tension. In crisis situations whatever you choose to do does not seem to bring any more control to the crisis at hand. The emergence of authority and leadership roles in a crisis is paramount, and the two staff members who responded first, Mary and Arlene, did the right thing in the emergency, calling Campus Security and keeping students calm until Campus Security arrived. Once Campus Security was on the scene, the established supervisory or administrative roles were superseded; in any event the head of the Taylor Library was unavailable as was the circulation supervisor (another example of systems failing).

What was not recognized in this case is that there are also principles of organizational justice that operate in crisis situations. The research of Harvey and Haines pointed out that it is not just *what* management does during a crisis but *how* decisions are made and communicated that is critical in determining how positive or negative the reactions will be to the crisis situation.[2] These reactions can affect work attitudes such as job satisfaction and organizational commitment. Looking at the facts of this case, it is clear that all the effort was focused on *what* to do and not enough attention was paid to the *how* of what was being decided or communicated. Decisions were made in Library Administration and then primary communication was with the staff seemingly most affected—the circulation staff in the Taylor Library. Although other staff were notified about what had occurred, they were not considered to be in danger, and as a result they were out of the focus of the activity relating to decision making and communication. Their feelings simmered until they found an outlet in the reluctance to work evening shifts. At that point none of the rational arguments were heard. All staff members knew what to do in event of emergency; it was their feelings and perceptions of safety and security that had not been acknowledged.

Moving forward from this experience has been difficult. It has taken a lot of time to dull the edge of feeling. I would argue that most staff feel safe working in the library most of the time, but it will never be the same. And none of us really wants the opportunity for a "do-over."

NOTES

1. Center for Creative Leadership, "Crisis Leadership: Making a Difference When Disaster Strikes; When Plans Fail, Improvise," *Leading Effectively* (January 2008), http://myccl.ccl.org/leadership/enewsletter/2008/JANplans.aspx.
2. S. Harvey and V. Y. Haines III, "Employer Treatment of Employees during a Community Crisis: The Role of Procedural and Distributive Justice," *Journal of Business and Psychology* 20, no. 1 (September 2005): 53–68.

MICHAEL CRUMPTON

10

A Phased Approach to Creating Updated User Spaces

THIS CASE STUDY WILL TELL THE STORY of how one academic library planned and created new library spaces over a period of ten years with limited resources but tremendous need to address multiple areas. Affordability was a primary concern, forcing a phased approach to renovations with a need to prioritize several issues, understanding that every penny counted and that it was important to truly assess and connect with stakeholders as each priority was considered. Academic libraries have been under pressure to move away from being warehouses for materials and to reinvent themselves into more user-centered institutions. "What does this mean for the spaces that libraries occupy, and how does that relate to adding value and relevance to the larger institution?" has become a common question for academic libraries in pursuit of remaining relevant.

The future of library spaces will lie in the ways users and stakeholders have changed and in what attributes hold value for them, both individually and as a group. Many of these changes involve offering patrons choices related to their use of space and providing a flexible, inviting environment for accomplishing their goals. Although our changes were limited financially over these ten years, making these changes gradually has the advantage of engaging users along the way to ensure that decisions made in the present will also support the future or provide a foundation for future growth.

This case study offers a view of renovating a library in phases, with the intent of not only updating spaces for current needs but also providing appropriate spaces in the future. Building and renovating these areas gradually allowed for continuous improvement as well as an analysis of what was learned in the process of assessment and environmental scanning in order to anticipate future directions.

OUR BEGINNINGS

"Arrangement provides flexibility, with ample areas for staff work and full service to college community." These words were written by the dean of the University of North Carolina at Greensboro, then called Woman's College, in December 1948. He was describing the new library building being constructed at the college and which is still the main library. When it opened in 1950, the library became a showcase for college librarians and architects, with the dean himself being considered a recognized expert on college library construction. This beginning and the influence of the dean impacted how academic libraries were viewed as learning spaces within the region for years to come.

Since those humble beginnings, the library has grown and changed in many ways, trying to keep pace with a burgeoning campus community and investing in developing a collection that supported the mission of not only the college but also the surrounding community. Growth of the campus and expansion of library services began almost as soon as the doors to the library opened. Development and expansion of campus program offerings, higher professional degree opportunities, and the transition from Woman's College to the University of North Carolina at Greensboro (UNC Greensboro) significantly impacted the library in holdings and status. A nine-story book tower, connected to the main library building, opened in 1974, providing space for a growing collection along with enhanced services and allowing librarians and staff to move forward with professional activities and program development to support the university's mission.

THE LEGACY INSTITUTION

These two distinctly different buildings—the main library and the book tower, connected across the first floor—were built before the introduction of the Internet and the proliferation of personal electronic devices. Updates to building codes were grandfathered in many cases, leaving the infrastructure static, and esthetic offerings were not prioritized, leaving little room for different uses of the space or critical review to improve services. In the twenty years following the opening of the book tower, the library focused on material acquisition, and the resulting space considerations became largely an effort to maximize physical content. While the organization was focused on acquiring more physical materials and resources, the introduction of computers and other technology in the 1990s brought new challenges to the building's infrastructure (power, HVAC, etc.). Changing material formats required special housing or equipment for access, and the Internet, in addition to having an impact on access to resources, revolutionized how users sought information, modified study habits, and transformed research processes. To accommodate some of the changes, a variety of small modifications of select spaces occurred, but it became increasingly clear that major changes needed to happen.

A constant factor in the history of the library is its fulfillment of a significant need within the university community: to support students. Students needed and used the library to further their educational experience and to fortify the skill set needed to succeed in life. However, foot traffic to the library was decreasing even before the advent of computers, and the library was seen as the legacy of a bygone era—a solid and stable institution, but too old and too outdated for current student needs.

As the academic community on campus grew, the library tried to keep up with students' research needs. Space for collections was expanded in the 1990s, but space for housing archives and accepting manuscript collections soon became full, while space for students to study and gather for collaborative work was reduced to accommodate more runs of shelving. By the early 2000s librarians realized that the library needed to revisit space priorities and update organizational needs as they related to fulfilling the library's mission to support the academic needs of the campus. Driven by the changing needs of students, library administrators recognized the need for a large-scale update. A survey in the June 2006 issue of the *Chronicle of Higher Education* listed having a good library as the second most important reason identified by prospective students for choosing a college. Armed with this information, library administrators became motivated to revisit our status on campus and move forward from our legacy reputation.

In 2006 library administrators developed a list of future space design needs in accordance with changing user expectations. This discussion evolved from the following facts:

> From 1974, when the book tower was opened, to 1995, when the tower reached its peak capacity of materials for which it was built, twelve thousand linear square feet of shelving was added to tower floors along with a remote storage facility outfitted with compact shelving that reached capacity by late 1999.

> The Special Collections Department was at capacity and could not accept major gifts or manuscript collections from potential donors.

Since 1995, seating capacity for students had been reduced by 50 percent to fulfill the needs of the growing collection. By 2005 student traffic had begun to increase again as students sought computers and equipment provided by the library. By 2008 we had seen a 42 percent increase in gate count, and the 14,648 square feet of common user space, which included lobbies, foyers, and hallways, were not enough. We also realized that staff work areas and active service points were inadequate.

Student study options and, in particular, group student space and labs were limited, in contradiction with the growing trend for students to study more in groups and use technology in a group-study mode.

The student population had increased at a faster pace than originally predicted, and this meant that with more residents living on campus, the need for library space increased as students needed more space for interactions and academic work.

The library undertook an interior upgrade project in 2005 and once again became an inviting place for students to study and spend time for a variety of reasons, but the upgrade was focused on esthetics and did not increase capacity.

The library had created two unique collaborator spaces to help facilitate group study with the aid of commonly shared electronic devices. These spaces turned out to be in high demand by students, and the concept needed to be expanded to meet student need.

Another measure of change was the library's instruction lab, known as the CITI Lab, built with the book tower in 2001. This lab was used for library instruction classes and seated twenty attendees with computers for hands-on instruction. Average class sizes by 2010 were closer to forty, so the lab was unable to accommodate the need.

These facts, common to many academic libraries, reflect the changes in higher education that create both an impact and an opportunity for academic libraries to expand services beyond warehousing resources and to create functional, inviting spaces that support curriculum.

CREATING THE VISION TO CHANGE

To be the university's library of the future, it was important for us to gain perspective about what was wanted and needed to be. And within the professional literature, it was not uncommon to see other academic libraries researching and investigating ways to make the change from being legacy institutions to being actively involved in the learning activities on campus and creating collaborative knowledge opportunities.

In a paper presented at the "Visions of Change" conference at California State University (CSU) at Sacramento in January 2007, David Lewis outlined a new model for academic libraries that would address current needs over the next twenty years.[1] Based on what was known at the time about changes to the profession and technology, Lewis's assumption for this model wrapped professional values around the need for physical changes to keep academic libraries in line with developments at their home institutions. Paraphrased, those assumptions were the following:

> Libraries are a mechanism to provide a means, not an end, for knowledge creation. Mechanisms must adapt as needed to be able to subsidize information and knowledge for end user needs.
>
> Disruptive technologies will drive changes in libraries, and libraries must recognize this shift and react appropriately to ensure continued support.
>
> Real change must be deep, at foundational levels, in order to sustain the purpose.
>
> Libraries have a historical and cultural significance that provides a window of opportunity to make changes that keep this connection, but that window will not always exist if it is not nurtured and properly maintained.

One component of Lewis's model was space. Specifically, he called for the redevelopment of the library into informal learning space, equipped with the needed attributes and infrastructure to satisfy the needs of informal learning. Many models now exist because academic libraries have worked collaboratively to identify the needs of students and to stay in touch with changing learning styles, new instructional methods, and new expectations for how the library supports the educational experience.

At the same time, some students expect the library to be their haven for quiet study, protected from the noise of dormitories, student centers, and other high-traffic areas. These students and those serious researchers need a library designed for study, research, and reflection. The library is no different now than earlier in seeking to serve the diverse needs of students and faculty, individually or en masse.

About 2005, early initiatives at UNC Greensboro to spur changes that supported the development of a new learning environment included the creation of "collaboratories," offering enclosed group-study areas with technical support, implementation of a 24/5 schedule during fall and spring semesters to allow round-the-clock access to the physical building, and allowance of food and drink in the building to give students an opportunity to work and multi-task in the library as they would in other places.

Space and resource limitations, however, caused these early efforts to fall short of what our campus needed. As a result, the constraint of available space became a grave concern about our future ability to serve students and faculty properly. The library administration determined that a large-scale assessment was needed to help guide future initiatives and investments for a new generation of learners.

THE CHANGING CLIMATE FOR ACADEMIC LIBRARIES

Considering the academic library as a pseudo environment for future professions, addressing the ways libraries as learning spaces impact learning activities is useful for understanding student needs as space needs to be renovated. The professional literature has addressed changes occurring in higher education along with related pedagogical activities occurring on campuses and has provided many examples of factors to be considered by academic libraries seeking to update and modify their spaces.

As these changes occur, traditional methods of providing space for services and resources stewardship have given way to a deeper focus on learning attributes and ways in which the library can play a significant role in non-classroom learning. With regard to spaces created for learning, we considered the following attributes from a report prepared for the Scottish Funding Council in 2006 concerning how learning occurs as we planned our renovations:[2]

> **"Learning through reflection:** *Studies into cognitive science have demonstrated that individuals who have the opportunity to reflect on information, to evaluate their own learning process and to identify for themselves new directions for study, are more effective. Learning through reflection is by necessity a solo activity."* For us, this attribute reinforced the need to maintain an element of quiet space as well as provide private opportunities for students to study alone and undisturbed.

> **"Learning by doing:** *Originating with seminal works by Piaget in the 1950s there is now much evidences that actively engaging in and working through practical tasks can assist learning. This might include computer-based simulations or physical simulation of real life environments. Learning of this type can include both group and solo activities."* This attribute demonstrated much of what we perceived to be changing in the classroom and encouraged us to consider more open spaces with tools and equipment (e.g., portable wipe boards) for students to be active. This concept

also laid the foundation for plans for a Digital Media Commons, discussed later in this chapter.

"Learning through conversation: *Central to the theory of social constructivism, learning from active discussion with teachers and other students is an incredibly effective way of improving learning outcomes. Learning through conversation is by necessity a group activity."* This attribute motivated us to consider collaborative needs related to group work and thus drove the design of collaboratories and other group spaces equipped with technology to facilitate group collaboration.

These ideas, with early consideration of changes in teaching methods, became the foundation for assessing what twenty-first-century students need as they prepare for professions that are also changing in our increasingly complex society. We knew that assessment was a critical component for providing the evidence needed to provide funding for shifting paradigms. To this point, our assessment had consisted of in-house surveys and discussions with students, but it was time to seek a professional point of view.

SPACE ASSESSMENT STUDY FOR THE LIBRARY

In 2008 a study was conducted with a designer and then matched and assessed with stakeholders to establish a priority of renovation projects as finances permitted over time for the main campus library. With each component, project assessment activities were engaged in order to identify and react to changing space needs. This approach established a "trend of changes" to library space with data and perspectives that informed future space needs. This assessment was important in order to link desired learning outcomes to renovation designs and operational concerns, keeping in mind that, strategically, decision making was impacted by political and economic factors, as acknowledged at the Learning Spaces Colloquium in 2011.[3]

The space assessment study, conducted by a local architectural firm, provided recommendations for the use of space at the library over the next ten years, before an expected library addition that was included in the campus master plan. The goal of the study was to identify appropriate changes in existing spaces to accommodate growth and expanding service and materials needs. Specific attention was given to the following:

People-oriented spaces and service points, including additional group-study space, individual study options, additional collaboratories, and other requested service needs as demonstrated through assessment measures

Expanded options for specialized materials such as archives, special collections, and government documents, with an assumption that remote storage options are available for lower use and duplicated format items

Increased space dedicated to instructional use in order to accommodate larger classes needing research skills instruction

Better use of existing areas that have traditionally not met their full potential or for which the purpose has changed since original conception

This study, completed in May 2008, featured a programming phase in which library faculty and staff provided input as well as two presentation meetings in which ideas presented were discussed and feedback collected. The space consultant also employed architectural design specialists who had library experience, structural engineers who were able to evaluate the technical requirements needed, and mechanical engineers who could determine whether infrastructure components (electrical, data, and plumbing requirements; HVAC; etc.) could support the recommendations.

The final recommendation was packaged, as requested by the dean of University Libraries, in five phases that would cost approximately $1 million per phase to implement. Because the library would need to find funding for this project, a phased approach would allow the changes to be addressed in steps. These steps could be linked but would still be considered separate pieces of a master vision for updating the aging structure into spaces that inspired learning and met the goals established earlier for space needs.

These recommendations affected each floor of the main building and the first two floors of the book tower. The recommended work also accounted for future anticipated construction and proposed student traffic changes throughout the building. In total the recommended changes would provide the following:

- Increased space available for users in both individual and group-study activities, adding approximately fourteen thousand square feet to double current capacity
- Opportunities to enhance services and provide better access for students working at nontraditional times
- Expanded space allocated to Special Collections and University Archives
- Space to house a larger instructional lab to seat at least forty students per session
- An alternative location for the print government documents collection
- Recommendations for people-oriented spaces and service points that would include additional group-study space, the Digital

Media Center, the Data Services Center, current periodicals, microform readers and materials, and electronically supported group and meeting space

A separate initiative was being developed by administration to obtain additional remote storage space in order to free current library space of low-use items and allow the expansion of new services and materials needs. The library space assessment included specific recommendations related to the removal of materials and to remote storage options that would be needed because of materials displacement.

It should be noted that although the architects did work with library staff on the programming needs for the organization, other assessment activities related to students and faculty were conducted by library staff to recognize the end users' desires and their use of the space. Assessment methods such as surveys, observations, focus groups, and individual interviews were employed to bring all the stakeholders into the project. Summarized findings indicated that students valued space over materials and that variety and flexibility were needed for space, furniture, and aesthetic options.[4]

THE LIBRARY RENOVATION—SCOPE OF WORK

Because of the 2008 recession and uncertainty about the status of future monies for additional renovation phases, phase 1 of the renovation represented a modified version of the May 2008 Space Assessment Study and incorporated desired elements from phases 1 and 2 of the original study. For this reason, fixture, furniture, and equipment responsibilities were removed from the project for the library to address on its own.

Conceptually, the following were identified as priorities for phase 1 with limited funding:

> Renovate the vacated third floor (main building) area to provide archive space for the library's Special Collections. Third floor work includes evaluation of the floor structure, repairs to the exterior windows, installation of a new HVAC system, electrical improvements, and a new fire suppression system.

> Provide or renovate offices, a small reading room, and a storage space in the same area for staff use.

> Renovate the basement level (main building) so the library can relocate the Government Information and Data Services Center, newsroom and study space concepts, and a library storage area.

> Modify the basement main stairwell access.

> Evaluate building code and accessibility code issues and incorporate required improvements as part of the project.

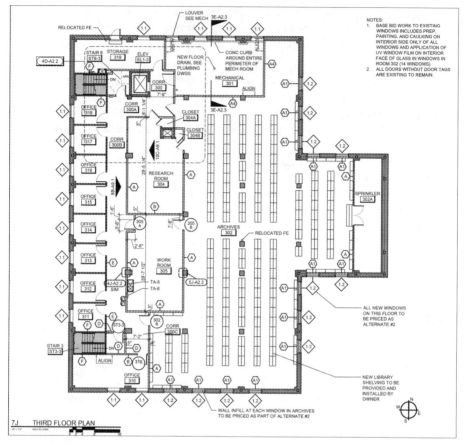

FIGURE 10.1

Third floor plan

This new phase 1 was completed in 2010 and provided significant improvements to the Special Collections and University Archives Department for the library. But it also set the stage for our realization of what we could do in steps without a major, overall building expansion or renovation. So completing this phase was significant for the motivation of forthcoming efforts. And the work on the phase itself was significant for showcasing the kind of impact that renovation can have on older spaces. Figure 10.1 is the drawing of the completed third floor in the main building, which, before renovation, was an open, empty storage area.

This area now provides environmentally appropriate space for collections, meeting and work space for projects and activities, and office space for staff whose work includes processing and collection configuration. It also allows space previously used by staff to be developed for another need—space for research and scholarly activity.

DESIGNING THE RESEARCHER SPACE

The library in recent years has seen explosive growth in its archive and manuscript collections as well as in other areas of Special Collections. Space was identified for repurposing and expanding these areas, and an assessment was conducted to identify the important attributes that needed to be addressed from a researcher's perspective. The Special Collections and University Archives Department was visited frequently by students, faculty, university staff, and individuals from outside the university who were conducting research with materials owned by the library. With the renovation of the third floor described earlier, these visits became more frequent, and proper accommodations were needed to adequately provide these services.

An assessment was designed to identify the typical researcher's needs related to type of work and physical expectations, such as lighting, temperature, work space, and available equipment or tools. We executed an electronic survey of recent researchers that provided talking points in subsequent interviews of randomly selected researchers. Demographic information was included as well as the classification of internal or external, meaning the individual's affiliation with the university.

The following criteria were compiled from the assessment related to establishing new research space within the library:

- Access to needed documents and restrictions placed on use and viewing
- Access to online materials and to tools used during physical review of materials
- Available equipment or tools (copier, scanner, etc.)
- Level of service expected relating to knowledge of materials, policies and authority control, and privacy issues (important for staff adjacency impact)
- Comfort features such as lighting, seating, table space, noise control, and temperature
- Logistical issues such as hours of operation, security, signage or locating information, and allowance of personal possessions

All these factors were critical for creating an environment conducive to productive research in our Special Collections Department. It was important to upgrade space dedicated to researchers as an indicator of the continued growth and significance of the various materials we were collecting and curating.

The findings from the assessment activities were compiled and presented to the designers to incorporate into their drawings and schematics for the designated space. Some items that dealt more with policies and procedures were forwarded to the department for consideration in managing and operating the new space. An added value of this activity and the related examination of the space were learning how to better market the space and collections to internal university researchers as well as external researchers coming from the community or out of town.

THE LIBRARY ELEVATOR PROJECT

In 2012, as part of a campus repair and renovation initiative, the elevators at the library were renovated for the first time since their original installation—1950 for the main building single car and 1974 for the book tower cars. The three-car traction elevator group in the nine-story tower and the single-car traction elevator located in the 1950 four-story portion of the library were completely modernized and upgraded. Improvements included new solid-state microprocessor–based control systems, new hoistway motors, call operating systems compliant with the Americans with Disabilities Act, and upgrades to each elevator machine room.

This project occurred in several stages, with access to two of the three elevators in the tower being discontinued initially followed by discontinuing access to the third in order to facilitate the work. Staggered work ensured that patrons with accessibility needs, such as wheelchair access, were accommodated properly. Patrons were encouraged to use the stairways in order to access higher floors or move between floors in order to reduce wait time for the remaining elevator in service. A campaign to encourage stairway use included a contest called "I climbed the Library," the health benefits of which were promoted by a local county health organization. The four elevators were completed on time with no incidents, and they now provide a fresh (and quick) uplift to the experience of visiting the library.

LIBRARY OFFICE SPACE ASSESSMENT PROJECT

Library staff spaces needed to be reviewed and considered for upgrades as well, so in 2012 a plan was developed to address some of the issues for staff offices that had been impacted by previous construction activity. Some spaces were vacated on the second floor as part of the materials move for the third floor renovation project. The original intention was to move the Digital Projects Lab, which had been temporarily relocated off the third floor, into this space adjacent to its home administrative department. We learned, however, that this space did not have the appropriate classification for the required occupancy. The following were goals and requests regarding engagement of a space consultant to provide the best recommendations for the use of this vacated space on the second floor.

The purpose and scope of this project was to assess and identify the best options for the existing space and accommodate other changes that had occurred or were being planned. These were the priorities that needed to be accomplished:

> Conduct a programming exercise in order to find a suitable location for the Digital Projects Lab, keeping in mind future growth expectations with supporting infrastructure and appropriate attributes.

> Address the specifics of the vacated space and provide options for the best use of that space with needed modifications for egress or any issues related to occupancy.

> Identify areas of flexible space that could be used for special projects or short-term, grant-related projects for both people and materials.

> Consider options and recommend alternatives in terms of other changes or related rearrangement of other departments or functions.

> Provide cost estimates associated with recommendations so that budgetary concerns can be addressed.

Ultimately, with input from outside designers, an internal campus project was initiated that provided for a modification to the second floor of the main building, housing staff and services. The scope of the project was to place the Digital Projects Lab and its accompanying administrative department into renovated space that rejoined the Digital Projects Lab with the resources within the department. This arrangement called for extensive work to HVAC systems and to electrical and network ports as well as provision of partition-based furniture for staffing needs.

CREATION OF THE DIGITAL MEDIA COMMONS

At this point, the original five-phase plan from the 2008 study was off track because funding never met the expected levels. The next greatest priority, informed by that study, was to create a multimedia lab to help the library embrace new and emerging technologies, so the library sought funding to develop a multimedia center. Envisioned was a center that could support curricular needs of students in creating a variety of multimedia products, including video, advanced software for media editing, and podcasts. This project supported goal 3.5 of the university's strategic plan (2009–2014), which included the initiative "infuse critical thinking, communication and informa-tion literacy throughout the undergraduate curriculum (21st Century Skills)." Our research and environmental scans of similar uses of space revealed that students are increasingly required to produce media for their classroom assignments, so investment in modified space was justified. Furthermore, graduates of the university are expected to develop media in many profes-sions, and this center was seen as an opportunity to prepare them for future career requirements. A campus initiative called "Communication across the Curriculum" was planning to add digital communication to its services along with writing and speaking consultations in order to offer students "transfer-able skills for life, civic participation, and work in a global society."

There was, however, no technical support for media creation by students other than students in the Media Studies Department. This lack represented a major gap in essential services for twenty-first-century students. The mul-timedia center would follow the model of the university's Writing and Speak-ing Center by providing consultants to assist students and by including the appropriate equipment, software, and spaces needed for multimedia creation.

In fall 2009 a task force on campus had been charged with exploring the need for a multimedia lab for students at the university and the possibility of housing it in the library. The task force researched similar services at other regional libraries and peer institutions. We also researched what services were available at the university for students and conducted a needs assessment of students. This task force was comprised of and collaborated with experts on campus familiar with learning theories that applied to this special environ-ment in order to maximize the impact on the resulting effort.

This campus task force charged with expanding these options for stu-dents recommended that the lab be housed in the library. The space targeted for this new lab needed to be cleared of existing stacks, monographs, shelv-ing, and bound journals. Funding, although limited, was pooled from a vari-ety of resources to support an infrastructure upgrade with temporary walls, electricity, network drops, carpet, and paint as well as equipment and soft-ware. A full-service staffed area was needed as well as small rooms for video and audio editing, a presentation practice and consultation room, pods with workstations for collaboration, large LCD monitors for shared-display group work, format conversion equipment (e.g., VHS to digital), a gaming and visu-alization lab, and multimedia viewing stations. The space also included pre-sentation areas with soft seating, collaborative areas with white boards, the library's film collection, flat-bed scanning stations, color and large-format printing, and the microform collections.

The proposal called for this space to be staffed and supported by the Uni-versity Libraries, but it was recommended to hire media studies students to serve as consultants. The following services were to be offered:

- Assistance with creating and developing digital videos
- Assistance with technical use of cameras and filming techniques
- Digital video editing and production
- Image creation and manipulation
- Media transfer to digital format
- Locating and incorporating video
- Publishing to the Web
- Creation and development of podcasts
- Scanning
- Color printing
- Large-format printing

Among our peer institutions, eight of the sixteen libraries provide support for multimedia production in the library. The administrative model varies—in some cases it is supported by an information technology services department or by a teaching and learning center; in others it is supported by the library or a collaboration between the library and one of the other units mentioned.

The task force also examined services available at our university. The University Libraries check out media equipment including flip cameras, video recorders, voice recorders, and tripods to all UNC at Greensboro students and faculty. The Teaching Resources Center, located in the School of Education, checks out similar equipment for School of Education students and faculty only. The Media Studies Department provides a lab that is restricted to students majoring in media studies. The Information Technology Services (ITS) Department provides scanning services in the labs but no assistance with any multimedia. In summary, except for media studies students, there is no support for students to develop multimedia; thus, a campus-wide need was identified.

A survey was sent in February 2010 to 3,717 students. Of those, 835 responded for a response rate of slightly more than 22 percent. Of these respondents, 120 indicated that they had developed a video presentation for a class. Sixty percent of these respondents did so because the video presentation was required by the professor, while 28.2 percent decided a video was the best way to fulfill an assignment. Slightly over half (52.5 percent) used their own camera, and most of these used the movie mode of their standard digital camera. Seventy-eight percent of the respondents did not receive any assistance on campus, and 43.5 percent said that they had obstacles developing their presentation. Fifty-four percent said that they would have benefited from having assistance from an expert.

To determine the monetary needs for renovating the space once emptied, a budget was estimated as follows:

Equipment

- 15–20 computers (probably a combination of PCs and MACs): approximately $50,000
- Streaming media server: $25,000
- 2 scanners: $3,000
- 1 color printer: $1,000
- 1 large-format printer: $3,000
- 3–5 LCD monitors: $175 each
- Video to digital deck: $1,200
- Slide converter: $200

Additional Network Ports

- 20 drops at $1,200: $24,000
- Estimated $5,000 in electrical work

Software

- Final Cut Pro for 20 machines: $5,500
- Adobe CS-5: $598

Furniture and Temporary Walls

- Workstations, dividing walls, tables, chairs, soft seating including delivery and installation: $325,000

Total Estimated Budget: $444,373

Funding was found, and the ideas and research that indicated the need for support of digital literacies became our Digital Media Commons. Figure 10.2 shows the area to be renovated—the basement of the main building—in its cleared state, free of materials and shelving. The area to renovate was the 13,900-square-foot open area, adjacent to the lecture hall scheduled by the registrar's office for curriculum classes. The circled areas are the stairwells already modified for egress pathways from the previously mentioned construction on the third floor.

Figure 10.3 shows the same space that now houses our Digital Media Commons (DMC), opened in 2013. The success and popularity of the space have exceeded expectations and made a tremendous difference in students' perceptions of the library, as we learned through a variety of assessment exercises, faculty comments, and student feedback.

The Digital Media Commons even has its own mission statement: *The Digital Media Commons supports the 21st Century learning and curriculum goals of University of North Carolina at Greensboro and the University Libraries by providing the space, technology, resources, services and expertise to support the digital creation of multimedia projects* (https://library.uncg.edu/spaces/dmc/).

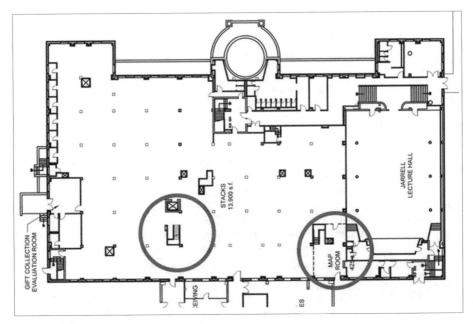

FIGURE 10.2
Area to be renovated

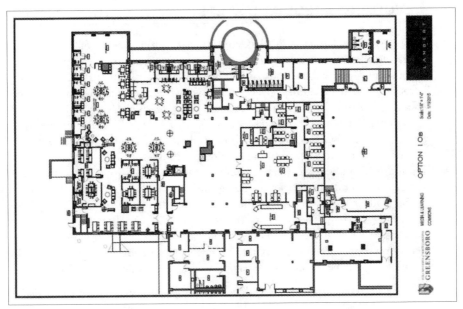

FIGURE 10.3
Digital Media Commons floor plan

In addition, goals were developed to establish focus on services and expectations from students:

> Provide interactive consultation services to University of North Carolina students, faculty, and staff in creating multimedia projects for their instructional and professional needs.
>
> Provide faculty development opportunities in creating multimedia assignments to develop students' information and digital literacy skills.
>
> Provide the space, technology, and expertise to shoot, edit, and screen films and other media, practice presentations, and collaborate on multimedia projects.

We have found that students use the DMC space and services to complete digital media projects that they cannot complete on their own, due to either technological or skill limitations. Students also use the DMC as a social place to study, complete group assignments, and practice presentations for class. Since opening, the DMC has added 3-D printing, a Video Imaging and Audio Lab (VIA) with a green screen wall, and a Gaming Lab. All these additions are meant to build an environment that supports connected learning through digitally literate products and services.

EVOLVING NEEDS ADD STEPS

As the student population has continued to grow, needs for collaborative seating, student work surfaces, and appropriate furniture for organized, and sometimes unorganized, discussion became apparent. The first-floor reading room in the main library was occupied by a variety of materials and services but was also a logical choice for expanding seating. Using concepts from *Designing a New Academic Library from Scratch,* an Ithaka S+R issue brief, we wanted to design space based on how students and faculty needed to use the room rather than on traditional opinions or thoughts.[5]

An Idea-Thon was held for library staff members to brainstorm and to discuss several approaches to space and service issues within the library. The reading room was one of the topic areas identified for scrutiny and was included in the presentation of the concept. Staff members shared a variety of ideas, observations, and what-ifs about this space in order to repurpose the reading room into a more inviting and usable space with higher capacity. The following is a list of the top items presented for consideration:

- Centralized and decentralized computer stations
- Tables for people in wheelchairs; adjustable computer desks
- Study and instruction rooms
- Big TV for news, weather, sports (e.g., the World Cup)

- Multifunctional—group and individual
- Physical limitations (wiring)
- Partition room by function
- Stationary and movable—no couches but clusters of chairs
- Tables to accommodate dual screens
- Signage on columns (vinyl letters)
- Wall colors to define function of space (furniture too?)
- Nothing bolted to floor (i.e., movable tables)

The ideas generated from the Idea-Thon were presented to student focus groups in order to better understand their preferences for the use of the room and how to create more efficiency for work and study activities without being too comfortable. Figure 10.4 shows the final layout that was agreed to by staff and students and that accommodates many of the desired elements generated in the Idea-Thon.

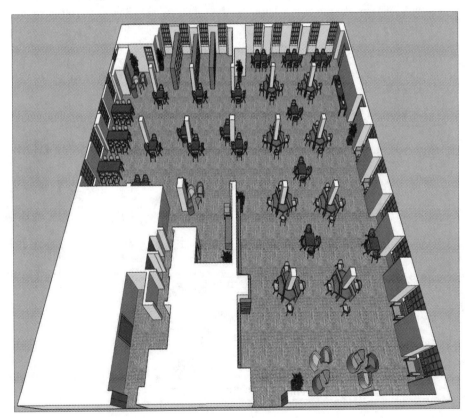

FIGURE 10.4
Final reading room layout and design

After these plans were finalized, vendors were brought in to develop furniture designs based on the information gained through the earlier processes. Two vendors familiar with our building attributes and limitations were selected to provide two different furniture types on different sides of the room.

Since completion of the refurbishment of the reading room, observation has shown high activity and multiple types of engagement, so the process and outcome have been considered a success. An additional element of this project was the provision of dry-erase boards. Although we have always had some available, for this renovation of the reading room we purchased large quantities and are seeing high use.

ENHANCED INSTRUCTION

One of the original goals for our phased approach to renovation was a larger instruction lab. The original library lab sat twenty, which was upped to twenty-five by exchanging some furniture for thinner desks, but average class sizes have grown closer to the forty to fifty mark. A larger lab was a needed priority and had not been addressed by earlier construction activity. The opportunity presented itself to portion off a section of the larger SuperLab, managed by the campus's ITS Department in the library, in order to make a larger instruction

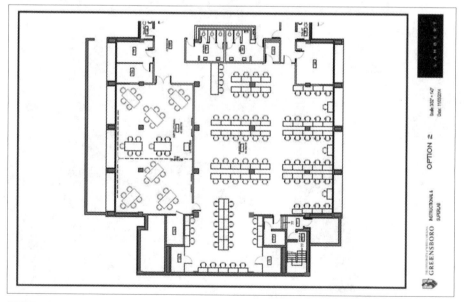

FIGURE 10.5

Final configuration of the instruction lab

lab. This lab adjoins the SuperLab and serves double duty by being open and available when classes are not being taught. Figure 10.5 shows this configuration with the closed-off instructional lab to the left of the larger general computer stations.

Factors considered for this project included maintaining the proper number of computers throughout the building that were open and available for general use and rerouting of infrastructure needs of the space to provide adequate HVAC, electrical, and data, along with safety protocols. This arrangement has worked out well and met all the goals for students needing computers and librarians needing instruction space. This was also a wonderful opportunity to collaborate with our ITS partners in providing computers and instruction to students.

CONCLUSION

Libraries today serve as a central hub on campus, a mecca for the social side of learning. Group-study assignments, combined with a higher technological expectation for the output of projects, can drive students into academic libraries with an expectation that the space and equipment will be able to accommodate those types of activities. Other expressed needs and desires for convenient services in the library are cafés, copy centers, and common interactive areas.

Our phased approach to renovating the library provided an opportunity to achieve improved learning spaces in segments, in lieu of a larger, full-scale renovation or expansion of the library. Our original 2008 space assessment study, although not executed as desired with five full phases to cover a broader assortment of needs, did inform changes made over subsequent years to provide improvements and needed upgrades. These renovations allowed our library the chance to enrich our students' learning and research opportunities for years to come and established the precedent that we can achieve smaller goals in smaller steps.

As academic libraries continue to be strong advocates for and conduits of information for their campuses, we are required to provide open and objective space for communicating, learning, and creating knowledge. Building or renovating smaller segments of space provides an opportunity to conduct assessment activities and engage stakeholders in order to best meet their needs, which helps our library approach our mission in a more integrated mode.

The growth of the university's student population, coupled with academic program development and our institutional mission for student success, required a common academic learning environment in which collaborative work and purposeful interactions can take place. The library's commitment to user-engaged learning informed the need for spaces that accommodate and support learning objectives and collaborative learning in a state-of-the-art, technology-rich environment, as discussed by Long and Holeton.[6] This commitment included making spaces available to support faculty research and instructional needs as well as accommodating members of the community and local partnerships. This renovation allowed the library to realize its vision as the information hub for the campus.

The issues that surrounded this work were complex but not insurmountable. Funding, always an issue, has changed our approach from what we anticipated from the 2008 study, but we were able to piece together needed funding for smaller projects from allocated funds, one-time considerations from campus administration, and unallocated funds from multiple sources. Establishing which priority to pursue next was also sensitive because different departments saw different needs and advocated for those. And the decision to assess stakeholders each time, although time-consuming, was valuable not only for determining details but also for communicating the intent of each project.

Across these years, the University of North Carolina at Greensboro's growth into providing higher level degrees as well as research-intensive activities has also added collections, services, and a complexity to user needs. These academic pursuits need a library that can provide common spaces on campus suitable for student collaboration and engagement as well as faculty and community interaction. In all other aspects, the library had the organizational capacity to support a growing and dynamic academic environment but was limited in execution by aged and inefficient space. Upgrading these spaces step-by-step gave us the opportunity to review learning design principles and to renovate space in a measured and informed way, helping keep the library a strong and relevant partner.

NOTES

1. D. W. Lewis, "A Model for Academic Libraries, 2005 to 2025" (paper presented at "Visions of Change," California State University at Sacramento, January 26, 2007).

2. AMA Alexi Marmot Associates in association with haa design, *Spaces for Learning: A Review of Learning Spaces in Further and Higher Education,* Scottish Funding Council Report (London: Alexi Marmot Associates, 2006).

3. M. A. Crumpton, "Having the Conversation: The 2011 LSC Colloquium," *Journal of Learning Spaces* 1, no. 1 (2011).

4. M. Crumpton and K. Crowe, "Using Evidence for Library Space Planning," in proceedings of the 2008 Library Assessment Conference, "Building Effective, Sustainable, Practical Assessment," Seattle, WA, August 4–7, 2008, 51–64.

5. N. Foster, *Designing a New Academic Library from Scratch* (Issue Brief), Ithaka S+R (2014), doi:https://doi.org/10.18665/sr.24776.

6. P. D. Long and R. Holeton, "Signposts of the Revolution? What We Talk about When We Talk about Learning Spaces," *EDUCAUSE Review* 44, no. 2 (March/April 2009): 36–48.

SARAH KEEN

11

Collaborative Digital Planning for Archives and Special Collections

Blue-Sky Thinking Meets Digital Projects Framework

UPSTATE UNIVERSITY WAS FOUNDED IN 1819 as a Baptist seminary and evolved into an elite liberal arts institution. The current student population is approximately 2,800. The university has two libraries—a main library housing humanities and social sciences materials and a science library—and nine departments total within those libraries. The libraries are staffed by sixteen library faculty (librarians and archivists), four administrative staff (two of whom have project appointments), and twenty support staff. The Special Collections and University Archives Department includes a Conservation Lab and is staffed by three library faculty, two project archivists, and one conservation technician; the department also employs several student workers. All department personnel joined the institution in 2010 or later.

When I joined the institution in 2010, the library had completed a few small-scale projects, mainly digitizing small image collections and a small run of a Chinese magazine, and was embarking on a long-term project to digitize student newspapers. In 2013, Special Collections outsourced a project to digitize the student yearbooks from 1883 through 2013; however, with the university's bicentennial approaching, the department was fielding more requests from university offices, faculty, students, and alumni for digital access to collections that had not yet been digitized. The requests also increased due to the improved access the department was providing to its collections by processing a thirty-year archives backlog, cataloging its rare books, and conducting more instruction sessions. The university administration supported an increased and improved digital presence for the department's collections, and the department felt that continuing its digital efforts served its mission to support the university's curriculum and to preserve and provide access to its collections. For example, digitizing the student newspaper allowed the department to discontinue access to the crumbling and unwieldy paper copies and enabled the full-text searching of 150 years of university history. The department had an ongoing, on-demand digitization program for individual duplication requests from researchers, but there was no overarching plan for selecting projects that would be undertaken in the future, especially large projects that would require intense staff and budgetary resources. With direct implications for funding, staffing, and infrastructure, the department needed to identify and plan digitization priorities for the next three to five years.

CREATING METHODOLOGY

Special Collections had never engaged in digitization planning before, and I was unable to locate a specific, documented process that suited the department's collaborative culture. Stitching together different methodologies, I created a process that the department used to think through the issues involved in planning and crafting a final report. Originally, the department set out to create a path for the next five years, though, as I will soon discuss, it was out of date within one year.

I learned one of the methodologies, called "blue-sky thinking," in 1999 during an undergraduate research internship at the University of Oklahoma for designing graphical user interfaces. For that project, participants were encouraged to express ideas without reservation or judgment with the intent of eliciting creative and novel thoughts. After everyone had contributed ideas, only then did we apply criteria to refine our options. The Special Collections Department adopted this methodology for brainstorming in order to allow for the inclusion of ideas that might at first seem impossible or far-fetched but that can come within reach given some creative thinking. This methodology would provide the broadest base on which to build future plans.

I also reviewed texts on strategic thinking, especially *Strategic Planning for Social Media in Libraries*. In the authors' discussion of planning your process and setting its tone, they make a critical point that has proven true in our swiftly changing arena of digitization priorities: "Your plan must encourage creativity and flexibility over rigidity. Because the plan will relate to an area that changes constantly, your attitude as a strategic planner must be one of preparedness for change."[1] At the time, the department was not expecting much change, and in an environment experiencing less change (or not preparing for an anniversary), it may not be as relevant. Planning the process and having a clear idea of what you want from the process are important, but the participants and audience for the final product should be prepared for change. Most strategic planning processes produce written plans of some sort, and I would make it evident that the plan is a framework and relevant given the circumstances at that time. If variables change, then the path may change as well.

In accordance with traditional strategic planning methods, the department conducted an internal SWOT (strengths, weaknesses, opportunities, threats) analysis. In researching other institutions' plans, the group came across the Claremont Colleges' Digital Projects Model[2] and used this as a structure for the SWOT analysis. The Claremont model breaks down projects into six components: people, hardware, software, metadata, materials, and money. If any one of these areas is weak, absent, or constantly changing, then a project's successful outcome is at risk.

Finally, the department incorporated an external scan into the process by considering who the primary users are and how they would use materials. Again, the book on social media and its discussion of audience proved useful in guiding this thinking. The authors ask you to think about what groups your organization serves and how they use the service in question (digital collections in this case). This list could be endless given the reach of the World Wide Web, but focusing on the top two or three groups could help focus the efforts in digitizing collections and developing the access platform. To streamline the process, the department did not include external participants during the meetings but did include their viewpoints through informal conversations that were held in the weeks leading up to the planning meeting.

PROCESS

To proceed with deliberations and discussions, the department needed to think about the tools that were used to accomplish its work. The personnel in the department tend to be visual thinkers, and it is useful to have shared content, so the group used sticky notes and whiteboards throughout the process. Sticky notes allow for individual reflection and generation of content that then can be shared with the group and categorized later as needed. You can reserve a particular color of sticky notes for thoughts that arise during a meeting but that may not be relevant to the topic at hand. These can be placed in what is often referred to as the "parking lot" for later use or discussion. The whiteboard (and a rainbow of dry-erase markers) allows for simultaneous generation of ideas within the group.

The department conducted a series of five meetings over the course of two months to discuss the various topics related to digitization planning. The first meeting was about creating criteria for deciding projects and setting tasks for the next meeting. The group reviewed the Claremont Colleges' Digital Projects Model as a means for generating criteria and used the whiteboard to record everything. The final report contained more refined phrasing, but the criteria by which the group assessed collections were as follows:

1. User needs
2. Material format
3. Availability of equipment needed
4. Availability of infrastructure to store and display digital objects
5. Costs
   a. Staff time
   b. Monetary
   c. What does not get done if particular projects are priorities
6. Curricular and teaching use
7. Level of research use, assessed through:
   a. Google Analytics
   b. Reading room use
   c. Duplication requests
8. Physical state of the materials

After the first meeting, each person was assigned to research the digital collections and platforms of a number of the university's peer institutions, as presented on their library websites. The group reviewed the findings at the fourth meeting and noted the variety of content included in pages described as digital collections. The group documented the benefits and drawbacks of the digital collections websites, with perhaps the most interesting aspect being the difficulty of locating the digital collection pages on many of the peer institution library websites that were investigated. This was a great example of learning from others' experiences and creating an ideal or goal to incorporate into one's own efforts. Overall, the review provided reassurance that the department's digital collections progress seemed to be on track with peers at other liberal arts institutions.

At the second meeting, the group used the blue-sky thinking method to identify collections for potential digitization projects. I began by explaining the technique and by emphasizing that all ideas were welcome and that participants should include whatever came to mind. Each person wrote down ideas on individual sticky notes. Including everyone in the department is important in this step, especially because each person has different interactions with the department's collections and patrons. Initially some participants did not feel that they had much to contribute because they did not provide public services and did not "know" the collections. However, this difference of perspectives allows for fresh views of what the possibilities could be. If a staff member did not have specific information about the department's collections, contributing ideas such as "beautiful bindings" or "collections that have striking images" was valuable.

After this brainstorming period, the group compiled the sticky notes and grouped any that were the same. Surprisingly, the overlap of ideas was minimal. Everyone nominated the general university photograph collection (currently the collection that generates the most image requests), and six other collections received two nominations each. Otherwise, the other twenty-seven suggestions were unique, emphasizing the variety of ways in which the department personnel see the collections based on their own work and their work with patrons.

For some institutions with bigger collections, this part of the process may seem like overkill or a useless exercise. For this department, it was important to surface new ideas and to engage each member of the department in contributing to the process. The moment of reviewing the sticky notes also allowed the group to share appreciation for the breadth of the department's collections and smile at the variety of possibilities for digitization projects.

The third meeting entailed brainstorming about the resources possessed by the department and the library in general and those that were needed or wanted. Assessing internal resources (people, equipment, materials, etc.) is a critical step for understanding what projects are possible to undertake without additional resources. This is also a good opportunity to appreciate all the tools already available. It is notable that two of the resources were "professors who want to collaborate" and "an audience that wants digitized materials." Such external resources are important for justifying programs and arguing for continued resources. One must be careful during the "assessing the gaps in resources" portion of the conversation because it can have a negative effect on your team's outlook (e.g., look at all the things we do not have!). For this reason, discussion of this topic should be facilitated carefully or delayed. I might remain with the positive and postpone identifying resources that might be needed to make specific dreamed projects a reality.

The fifth meeting involved assessing the department's drivers and environment. The group identified key questions first. Which users most need and use the library and collections? Which courses and majors most often use collections? What groups do we serve? Why are people using digital collections? For each of these questions, the group brainstormed a list of possible responses. The group also identified key drivers for the next five years, the main one being the university's upcoming bicentennial, and generated a list of additional questions that were kept in mind for further consideration (e.g., what collections are most useful to the bicentennial, and what might get used more if it were more accessible?). In addition, the group identified critical uncertainties regarding digital storage space, funding, personnel capacity, digital preservation, sustainability, and the overall goals and expectations of the library and university.

Using the criteria established earlier in the process, at the final meeting the group reviewed the list of collections gathered through earlier brainstorming and assessed each suggestion against these criteria. It quickly became evident that some collections and materials were beyond the department's scope or ability to digitize at this time due to lack of resources or lack of demand. The group prioritized those materials that received high use, those that were physically fragile or inaccessible due to format, those that were rare, and those for which the department received external digitization project requests. This process winnowed the list down to three categories of priorities that could be achieved over the next five years: in-house projects, vendor and outsourced projects, and collaborative projects. Given the work involved in collaborative ventures, this last category was more speculative than the other two, but it can be useful to include some possibilities that set the achievement bar higher.

FINAL PRODUCT

All our work culminated in a final written report that I composed for the university librarian, who had the opportunity to offer any comments or insights. The report provided her with a better sense of the resource needs for future digitization ventures should they be pursued. This particular edition of the report was not meant for dissemination to an external audience, but the content provided talking points for discussion with university administrators if needed. The greater value for this report was for my department and the libraries overall, so that we could plan more strategically for the next few years and devise ways of acquiring equipment, software, or expertise that was needed. Planning for increased digital storage space was a particular concern for the department's preparations to conduct audiovisual digitization because the file sizes are much larger than those for image files. In addition to resource planning, Special Collections could prioritize collections for processing or preservation in preparation for digitization. In addition, the department could better respond to external inquiries about digitization projects and communicate that plans existed to proceed with such a project or indicate that the idea would need to be deferred or that priorities would need to be reevaluated in order to take the project on.

As mentioned earlier, within one year, the plan was outdated. The department acquired new equipment that increased its in-house capabilities, but the members of the department also needed time to learn how to use that equipment effectively. In addition, the department experienced staffing variability that impacted our ability to manage vendor and in-house projects, thus delaying our time lines. With the university's bicentennial approaching, the digitization needs of external parties shifted from previous discussions, and the department had to take that into account and accelerate plans for digitizing audiovisual materials. With the rapid rate of change that many institutions experience, some might question the benefit of engaging in planning when the plans will be outmoded so quickly. The ultimate benefit for Special Collections was that the plan enabled an agile response to change and a quick reassessment of the resources that existed to address new priorities. Now the department personnel could quickly assess how the greater priority for digitization projects overall would affect the ability to proceed with other work in the department.

LESSONS LEARNED

Reflecting on the process that the department followed, several changes could be made if the group conducted such an extensive degree of planning again. A benefit of having the original plan is that Special Collections does not have to carry out an extensive process each year; rather, personnel can reflect on what has changed and update the plan accordingly. This opportunity for the department to reflect and make conscious decisions about its work in times of change is valuable and builds team cohesion and contributes positively to the department's climate.

Experiencing the process provides more confidence in enacting it and reflecting on specific activities that could be improved. The group conducted its five meetings over the course of two months, squeezing them in with other work. If Special Collections could conduct the process during one day as a retreat or during two half days, that approach would be preferable and help maintain momentum. The specific brainstorming activities used were meant to elicit novel ideas, and they served that purpose in this instance. Having attended a professional leadership institute and read new materials on group dynamics since this process, I would explore additional tools and methods that could improve the brainstorming process and diminish the focus on group-generated ideas and use of the whiteboard, which can favor the more outgoing or outspoken members of a group. More individualized or reflective brainstorming methods could draw on the strengths of the introverted members of a group, and using a variety of methods could take advantage of the strengths of all involved.

I describe the process as collaborative because everyone in the department worked together in pursuit of a shared goal, that of creating a plan for future digitization work. The methodology worked in this case due to the willingness of all personnel to contribute to the process, share their ideas in an open manner, and feel safe in doing so. In addition, the department already possessed a climate of open communication, so the collaborative process reflected the department's existing work style. Before undertaking this type of collaborative endeavor, the leader of the process would need to identify whether safety existed within the participating group or if work needed to be done to establish that safety.

Ideally the planning group would have included colleagues from the Library Systems Department who support library technology needs, but the library had key vacancies in that department at that time. With those vacancies now filled, Special Collections has involved those individuals in discussions of future digitization projects. The Special Collections Department's work has a direct impact on the Library Systems Department's budget and resources, because Library Systems is responsible for budgeting equipment needs and acquiring digital storage. Both departments also are working together to create digital preservation plans for the content that is digitized.

Early in the digital project planning process, the group made the decision to preserve the digital master files to reduce the physical impact of digitization on the original materials, and this decision is reflected in the department's image and text digitization guidelines. This practice is recommended in the special collections and archives professions so that when additional derivative files need to be created, they can be derived from the high-resolution master file, and the original object is not subjected to additional handling and light exposure. In addition, retaining and preserving the digital master files protect the resource investment made by the institution in digitizing its materials.

It can be difficult to lead a process if you are also an eventual participant and stakeholder as I was. I am the department head, but I am also involved in the projects and have a stake in ensuring their success. For future sessions, it could be useful to have a third party, such as a trusted colleague from another department or institution, lead the discussion so all can participate more freely. If this is not an option, it is important to acknowledge when you are speaking from your different roles and to make it evident when you are speaking as a leader and when you are speaking as a peer. Even when speaking as a participant, I was careful to frame my contributions as neutrally as possible given that I oversee the work of everyone in the department. The most important task for a leader in this type of process, though, is to listen to the contributions of everyone else and create a safe environment for open and honest sharing.

NOTES

1. S. K. Steiner and E. Kroski, *Strategic Planning for Social Media in Libraries,* THE TECH SET® #15 (Chicago: ALA TechSource, 2012), www.ebrary.com.
2. L. L. Crane, *The Claremont Colleges Digital Library: A Model for Digital Projects* (presented at Southern California Technical Processes Group, "Managing Digital Projects," University of San Diego, January 2011), http://ccdl.libraries.claremont .edu/cdm/ref/collection/adl/id/53.

12
Collaborating for Success

JEAN TIMMS* WAS SITTING IN HER OFFICE, carefully reviewing the notes she had prepared for her upcoming meeting with her supervisor. As a librarian who was used to being a subject specialist with few administrative duties, she was still figuring out how best to fill the management position she had found herself in for the past eight months. Like many information professionals, Timms had not pictured herself in a management role, or at least not at this point in her career. "Fake it 'til you make it!" is what one helpful colleague advised. Perhaps not the most eloquent piece of advice, but it got her through those challenging days when her confidence was not exactly soaring. The Wainwright School of Business, in which her library was situated, was teeming with bright minds, eager to tackle complex financial, strategic management, and organizational issues (in theory at least). They all seemed so poised, so self-assured. She often channeled that energy and youthful enthusiasm, and she had the good fortune of choosing an extremely competent and detail-oriented colleague for her small team. Vanessa Alfonso was just a few

* All names in this case study are fictional.

months out of library school but was already demonstrating a lot of initiative and drive.

A loud and almost anxious knock at the door startled Timms. Through the glass door, she saw her supervisor, Elaine Chen, smiling broadly. Elaine had arrived a few minutes early and was holding what looked like a spreadsheet and an e-mail printout.

So Chen was going to talk numbers today. "I can handle that," thought Timms, as she cleared off a space on the table and then took a large sip of her second morning coffee.

"I've got fantastic news for you, Jean," announced Chen, as she strode into the office. "The funding request that I submitted in February for more databases for the Business Library was approved! I'd like you to start looking into acquiring licenses for Bloomberg terminals. They're still the industry standard in the world of finance, and we need to get students on them now, to give them a leg up once they start their careers." Timms was momentarily flummoxed. She was used to researching databases for months before making any decisions about purchasing, especially because collections budgets had not exactly been generous in the past few years. But now here was Chen urging her to acquire what she guessed would be a fairly expensive tool. "This must be *really* important to have," she realized. She and Alfonso had a lot of work ahead of them to acquire and, more dauntingly, learn how to use the database, especially because they were not experts in finance databases. In fact, Timms cringed each time a faculty member or student asked a question about historical interest rates, revenues, or ratios. Worried, Timms thought to herself, "How should I go about gaining expertise on this matter when I'm clearly not in my comfort zone?"

BACKGROUND

The Wainwright School of Business, an institution accredited by several significant associations in management education, is located in a major Canadian city and serves more than four thousand undergraduate students and 260 graduate students. Founded in 1969, the school is part of the University of Stromville, one of the top ten research institutions. The university is focused on further building its research intensity. As part of the third-largest faculty on campus, the two embedded librarians found themselves quite busy providing information literacy instruction; covering the joint information and circulation desk, which included a heavily used reserve collection; purchasing some print but mostly electronic material to support undergraduate, graduate, and executive programs; and maintaining online research guides. All this activity meant there was little time for doing personal research projects, marketing the library's services, and conducting faculty outreach. Timms and Alfonso were a "small but mighty" team, and they enjoyed the busy-ness even though it was overwhelming at times, especially by October when they could be found giving two or three presentations a day in classes that ranged from Introduction to Business to Research Methodology and even more specialized courses like Electronic Business Technologies and Engineering Management. The students in the four-year bachelor of commerce program were by far their largest audience. There were several program options, including the opportunity to do a highly coveted co-op term, but the accounting and finance programs were among the most popular. These students were almost always guaranteed a good entry-level position in an accounting firm, a bank, or a government agency, especially with some practical experience under the belt. They had to compete with a lot of other graduates from more established and recognized institutions with business schools, such as McGill University and the University of Toronto, located close to the heart of the major financial districts in Canada.

Timms felt lucky to be working in the Business Library, a modern and elegantly decorated space that occupied a corner of the second floor of the business school. The area was filled with natural light and had a quiet study zone that was often packed with students searching for an oasis of calm. The library provided a few desktop computers as well as some comfortable chairs for lounging and for reading the business magazines and newspapers. Although most of the students brought their own laptops or tablets, they still came by the library to take advantage of the Wi-Fi in the building.

After Timms received her MLIS, she immediately set out to find full-time work in an academic setting that would offer many benefits, including continuous intellectual stimulation, support for professional development, and a chance to go on sabbatical after putting in enough years of service. She was ready to take on new challenges even if it meant learning an entirely new subject area. Although it was fulfilling to complete a liberal arts degree with a specialization in Romance languages in her undergraduate studies, she was not certain that accomplishment would help her achieve her life or career objectives. Hence, she decided to attend library school where she took as many reference courses as she could handle to get a better grasp on resources in a variety of disciplines.

The knowledge she built up over the years, along with her eagerness to carry out a variety of new and interesting duties, allowed her to get a foot in the door at the University of Stromville. She was also a team player, though like many introverts, she usually preferred to work alone. When she first found herself in a university library setting, she reluctantly recognized the fact that much work had to be done within a committee or working group. She often learned a lot from the other members of the team, but at times she wanted things to move much more quickly so that an action could be taken "right now" instead of according to a predetermined time line. "This meeting is interminable, and we're nowhere near consensus," she once whispered to the senior reference technician seated beside her during one particularly contentious meeting about the implementation of a new discovery layer for the library catalog.

Now that she had more than seven years of experience as a librarian, she had become much more patient and was learning to trust the tried-and-true processes in place to get projects going, realizing that there were usually layers of complexities to uncover, not to mention having to navigate office politics, "big" personalities, competing university priorities, and always, always the need to do more with less.

COINCIDENTAL CROSSROADS

When Timms filled in her colleague about the task at hand, Alfonso was keen to lend her support. "Let me know what you'd like me to start researching, and I'll get straight to it!"

"How about you start looking at which other business schools in Canada have these terminals so we can reach out to other librarians who have experience using Bloomberg?" instructed Timms. "I'll find a Bloomberg representative for our region and arrange a visit." Manny Triglione, senior account manager at Bloomberg for Eastern Canada, responded enthusiastically to Timms's request for a meeting and agreed to give a demonstration a week later. "Feel free to invite any faculty members, especially those in finance, who might be interested in hearing more about our product. After all, they're the ones who will likely be using it in their classes and for their research," Triglione boomed over the phone.

The one-hour presentation that Triglione gave for Timms and the six professors who had responded to her call for participation was very slick and well rehearsed, though the faculty members did not seem entirely convinced. "Having Bloomberg embedded in the curriculum here at the Wainwright School of Business will completely change the way that students access financial and company information," said Triglione. "And remember that if students take the Bloomberg certification, they can include it on their résumé."

"He's making some great points here," noted Timms. "I better remember to let the Career Center staff know about this as well." Little did she know that Cory Minten, a career counselor with an avid interest in finance, had already been in touch with Triglione because he was in the midst of developing a new financial markets mentorship program intended for upper-year Wainwright students. "What a crazy coincidence!" Timms said to Minten as they chatted in the hallway the day after the presentation. Not only was Minten thoroughly set on getting this research tool, but he was envisioning an entire trading lab! Clearly he was of the "go big or go home" mind-set.

When Timms touched base with Chen at their next meeting, the librarian filled in her supervisor about the progress of the information gathering and noted that another person had a vested interest in Bloomberg—Minten. "Well," said Chen thoughtfully, "this is a perfect storm—a chance to leverage his program and the internal stakeholders at Wainwright to push to get these terminals in place. Although our collections budget can cover the cost of the tool, you'll need to focus your energies on getting buy-in from faculty to actually *use* it. We do not want an expensive terminal sitting around collecting dust. Why don't you arrange another presentation to faculty and invite the Bloomberg rep again?"

Timms got to work arranging this follow-up presentation, which was fairly straightforward because she and Alfonso had worked tirelessly on gathering details not only about trading labs, their use in Canadian universities, and the various tools found within these spaces but also about which courses could benefit the most from Bloomberg. In the end, the two librarians had a clear idea about which Canadian universities they could pinpoint for further support because Alfonso had created a table outlining the schools that had a Bloomberg terminal, a trading lab, or both. To the librarians' surprise, they found that of the forty universities with business schools, twenty already had either this tool or a lab! On presentation day, the slide showing those numbers proved to be the most provocative one.

"What are we waiting for?" cried Professor Orlea, one of the more outspoken finance professors at the school. "We can't compete for the best students if we don't have this tool in place!" Orlea also happened to be a great champion of the library, so Timms was quite pleased to hear her reaction. She had already pinpointed the argument that the tool could help improve "student experience," which was one of the university's strategic objectives. Triglione's Bloomberg demonstration was once again dazzling, but it was the research that Timms and Alfonso had provided that stayed in the minds of the professors.

NEXT STEPS

When the dean's office learned about this presentation through various interactions with the finance professors—interactions that included spirited hallway discussions and tersely written e-mail messages—staff reached out to Timms for further details. "Jean, I want to know more about what happened at this presentation," wrote Dean VanderNoot. "My secretary will set up a meeting next week. It sounds like we need to start talking about building a trading lab again."

"Again?" thought Jean. It turned out that there had been discussions many years ago about the development of a finance lab, but the priority then was to find funding for a new building for the school.

"That plan dropped off our radar because we were focused on much bigger issues at the time," explained Tom Daignault, the facilities manager for

Wainwright. Timms found herself seated at the mahogany boardroom table between Daignault and Bill McDuff, the vice dean for external relations who was responsible for many of the fund-raising initiatives at Wainwright and was colloquially known as "the Money Man." Thankfully Chen was at the meeting as well to help provide details about library support. Timms was relieved that her supervisor was there to back her up. She was usually confident in representing the Business Library, but it was a pretty big deal to be at the table with some of Wainwright's top people. It was nice to see another familiar face who had many more years of experience with these kinds of meetings and with project planning. Professor Orlea was also in attendance and flashed Timms a thumbs-up sign as she settled into a chair right beside the dean. Minten was invited but had a prior commitment, so his manager was there to represent his interests.

Dean VanderNoot welcomed everyone and quickly set the agenda. "We're going to need to work together to get this lab up and running. Do we have enough information about what goes into these sorts of labs and some approximate costs?"

Chen jumped in to respond, "Jean and Vanessa have done a lot of legwork in researching finance labs. They even talked to several contacts at labs in the United States and Canada and had a chance to visit a few in Montreal. I understand that Cory has also visited some sites and got some firsthand knowledge."

"Yes, that's right," exclaimed Timms. "Based on all the information that we gathered, we know that this is going to be a major investment for the school and the library, but one that is necessary to stay competitive. We found that there was quite a spectrum of labs out there from basic to cutting-edge. We'll have to decide among ourselves what our concept should include."

One by one, each person around the table chimed in with an opinion, a comment, or a question. Everyone agreed that this space had to be built but

Short-term: Spring 2012	Phase 1: September 2013	Phase 2: September 2015
2 Bloomberg terminals in Business Library	9 computers + contract lab manager + volunteer student assistants + more licensed resources	30 computers + lab manager and assistants (2 FTE) + student assistants + group-study rooms

FIGURE 12.1
Finance lab time line

that funding it was going to be a real challenge, even for a small lab. McDuff had a few leads in mind for sponsors, though there was no concrete money in the coffers for this initiative.

After several meetings through the fall and winter, this working group decided that taking a phased approach would be the most realistic path (figure 12.1). But one thing was not yet entirely clear to Timms: who was actually going to "own" this lab—the Business Library or the School of Business?

TWO TREASURED TERMINALS

In the weeks that followed the successful presentation, the librarians developed a plan to get the terminals into the library because there seemed to be no other place within the business school that could hold them. This arrangement would mean that the team had to learn the ins and outs of Bloomberg before they could confidently market it to students and faculty members. "Thank goodness for all the tutorials that are already out there. No use reinventing the wheel," thought Alfonso, as she uploaded links to the growing list of resources on the Bloomberg research guide that she was developing.

While this preparatory work was taking place in the library, Minten at the Career Center was arranging a financial markets competition for his group of students, one of the key personal objectives he had in mind for that year. "It won't work without the Bloomberg terminals though," he worried. "I'll have to let Jean know that my time line's pretty tight. They *must* be available by March 15 or else this competition will be a bust. I've been developing this competition with Triglione's input for a while now. Those reps really know their stuff!" He thought about writing a friendly but firm e-mail to Timms, then decided that an in-person meeting would be more convincing. Striding over to the library with cell phone in hand, Minten smiled to himself as he imagined the title of the press release that would follow the event: "First Annual Capital Markets Competition: A Booming Success!"

UNDER PRESSURE

With the help of the electronic resources team, the information technology (IT) technicians from the library's systems team, and the Wainwright IT staff, and after much back and forth with customer service representatives at Bloomberg, the two terminals were finally set in place despite a few technical glitches. "I wish we could afford more than two right now because I'm pretty sure the demand for these will be insane, especially with this upcoming competition," worried Timms. She and Alfonso had devoted a good part of the winter term to making sure that the Bloomberg terminals would fulfill the hype that had been built up about them. Not only was there growing interest in Minten's mentorship program, but now a few faculty members from economics and mathematics had got wind of the powerful tool through their library representatives. Timms and Alfonso realized that their colleagues needed to know about this resource as well, especially the liaison librarians for related disciplines and the staff who worked at the main reference desk. Word usually spread quickly on campus about "cool tools" that had tons of data and functionality. "We'll use an online booking system to manage reservations. That should help control use and will help us keep stats on use, too," figured Timms.

MEETING MADNESS

In the usually slower spring term of the academic year, Timms could have been planning which library conferences to attend that year to continue her professional development, but instead she found herself in more meetings than she ever thought imaginable. Miraculously, the School of Business managed to secure the space within the building to start construction of the lab, so Timms was in full planning mode, with a focus on budgeting. With Alfonso's guidance (her project management skills were a lot stronger), Timms created a template to fill out the costs over the next three years and had meetings lined up with vendors, facilities staff, and even the library's chief administrative officer to get some hard numbers (figure 12.2). "Thanks, Vanessa! This should help us get a ballpark figure for the lab, but I'm anticipating a lot of other requests from students and faculty," said Timms. She remembered Chen's words of wisdom: "You won't be able to please everyone, Jean. Just do your best to get all the essentials set up, then we can work together to find pockets of money from all our partners."

FAST FORWARD TO FALL LAUNCH

Join us at the official launch event for the expanded Financial Lab!
We are pleased to announce the launch of the newly expanded Lab, which will be opening this fall. The Lab will be a state-of-the-art facility three times its original size and offer students access to more computers equipped with finance databases such as Bloomberg and other analysis and research tools, in order to better meet its increasing demands. The expansion of the Lab is part of the library's and the Wainwright School's ongoing commitment to student experience and to accounting and finance research and pedagogy.

	UNIT PRICE	NO. OF UNITS	YEAR 1	YEAR 2	YEAR 3
Other					
Data					
Electrical					
Wall-repaint					
Ventilation					
Furniture/Hardware					
Desks					
Chairs					
Computers (4GB of memory required)					
Bloomberg Keyboards					
Monitors (2 per computer)					
Computer Software					
Microsoft Office Suite					
SPSS					
Teaching Station					
Computer or Laptop					
Podium					
Peripherals					
LED TVs					
Cable subscription					
Speaker system					
World Clocks					
Research/Data products					
Bloomberg					
Rotman Interactive Trader (trading floor simulation software)					
Capital IQ					
Trading Games					
FactSet					
TOTALS					
Staff					
FT Lab Manager					
Chair					
Desk					
Computer					
TOTAL					

FIGURE 12.2
Finance lab budget template

Timms read the e-mail invitation with pride and satisfaction. It had been less than five years since she and Alfonso had first become involved in the lab's development. There had been lots of hiccups along the way, and the constant need to find sources of funding had been stressful, but it was worth it. Now she was supervising a full-time lab manager who had quickly built up the reputation of the lab, helped to integrate its resources into many courses (some faculty members were still lukewarm about the lab even though Orlea had continuously supported its development), and organized competitions in which the school was quite often ranked among the most elite b-schools in the United States and Canada. A talented and enthusiastic professional with finance experience and an MBA was at the helm, so Timms no longer worried *as much* about this space, which had successfully become a hub of activity for the hundreds of Wainwright students specializing in finance. She and Alfonso could now focus on some of the other emerging developments at the school, including new graduate programs and the hiring of several new faculty members, not to mention keeping up with the usual demands on their time and the new literature review search service they had launched two years ago.

Timms enjoyed overseeing the lab, though she sometimes wondered how her position really fit into the future of this space, which had quickly become prominently displayed in Wainwright's marketing and recruitment material. The library was footing the bill for the ongoing costs of subscription resources, but because these resources were some of the invisible assets of the lab, it was easy to understand why they were sometimes not credited in its success. During her latest annual review meeting, Timms had shared her concerns and feelings of mild frustration with Chen, who counseled her patiently: "Jean, there are many ways to lead a team, and it's not always from the front of the pack."

"Why is Elaine speaking to me so cryptically?" wondered Timms.

"Do you recall one of the books that I recommended you read many years ago when you first stepped into this role? *Becoming a Manager: How New Managers Master the Challenges of Leadership* by Linda A. Hill is a book that I return to many times throughout the year, even though I've been a manager for decades! Well, this same author champions the idea of 'leading from behind,'" Chen explained. "Take some time this summer to read more about this idea, then let's discuss it over lunch."

Timms left Chen's office intrigued and set off to do some research on this theory. When she sat back down at her desk, her eye caught the poem about leadership that she had pinned on her bulletin board years ago:

May you never put yourself at the center of things.

May you act not from arrogance but out of service.

(John O'Donohue,
"To Bless the Space between Us," 2008)

TWO STEPS BACK?

Over the summer, Timms was looking forward to reflecting on the vision of the lab and on how it could be further expanded. Her natural thought was to increase the suite of products available to students as well as researchers. Having somehow read her mind, some of the finance professors had already approached her and provided a long list of databases that they were keen on acquiring. But Timms's thoughts of going "bigger and better" were soon thwarted. After an emergency library management meeting attended by Chen, Timms received some crushing news. "Jean, the library's collections budget did not receive a cost-of-living increase this year, and as you know, our purchasing power has been greatly diminished with the drop in our Canadian dollar," Chen said soberly. "I'll do my best to protect the resources for the lab, but you'll still have to make some cuts—there's no two ways about it."

Although this was truly disappointing news for Timms, she knew this development would not necessarily spell disaster for the lab. After all, this new space was about much more than just providing finance data, wasn't it?

Questions for Readers

What issues should Timms consider to ensure a sustainable suite of specialized resources that respond to both student and faculty needs?

How can Timms promote and market the finance lab beyond the School of Business?

What measures should Timms take to maintain the relationships she built with the various stakeholders who helped create the lab?

What kinds of programming could the finance lab create in collaboration with the library to attract non-finance (e.g., entrepreneurship, marketing) students to the space?

During the spring and summer terms, the finance lab is underutilized given the relatively few finance courses offered. How can this space, including its costly resources, be optimized?

SANDRA VARRY

13

Engaging Internal and External Stakeholders in a Comprehensive University Archives Program

MOST COLLEGES AND UNIVERSITIES have archives and archivists, and most often these are part of the library of their institution. University archivists have a unique role as liaisons to all the departments on their campus as well as to their alumni and community in acquiring, preserving, and making available materials that have enduring historical value. What happens when the university archives are entwined with a separate, previously created program and several stakeholder entities? What about the sudden and unexpected management of a quasi museum? Although the Heritage Protocol and University Archives (HPUA) at Florida State University is in a unique situation, the elements of politics, facilities and human resources management, donor relations, and marketing and outreach are common to many academic library environments. During the evolution and expansion of such a multifaceted initiative, how do staff and stakeholders find the way to the other side? This case study highlights and discusses the challenges and strategies for library programs, such as university archives, in engaging with internal, campus, and community stakeholders to develop and manage a complex archives program.

University archives transcend physical collections in that they typically include elements of records management, serve as a liaison to departments, process unique materials, digitize, offer reference, perform outreach and marketing, manage facilities and human resources, and cultivate donors. Although some institutions have "lone arrangers" with limited versions of these functions, there are also entities with multi-person teams, including a full-time records manager. Many university archives are located within the library as part of a special collections department, or archives may be a parallel department in the library, or part of the university's administration, such as the department of finance and administration or the office of the president.

WHAT IS THE HERITAGE PROGRAM?

Florida State University had informally collected institutional records over the years and had an "archival materials policy" as early as 1978. However, the first archivist hired specifically to handle university-related material did not arrive until 2007, and even then the emphasis was on materials that represented the student experience. Until that time, Special Collections and Archives in the university libraries had frequently turned materials away, including alumni collections (scrapbooks, ephemera, etc.), due to the lack of space and other unknown factors. In addition, some records left the campus for storage at the state archives record center (storage for the retention period per state law) and then were deposited permanently or destroyed with little involvement by the university. Because of these circumstances there are large gaps in the breadth, depth, and diversity of the overall collection. Thus, the university has few records pertaining to our founding institution and the earliest site of higher education in the state, The West Florida Seminary (1851–1901), or to the Military Institute during the Civil War or to the Florida State College (1901–1905).

In 2001, in preparation for the university's sesquicentennial, staff, faculty, and alumni became frustrated with the lack of collections and interest in our earlier institutions, specifically the Florida State College for Women (1905–1947). A group of alumni, current and retired faculty, and staff mobilized to solve this problem as well as the lack of a clear commitment to collecting university history.

The first archivist who was hired stayed for about a year, with the successor staying on until 2013. Those initial student experience–based collections that were turned away by the libraries were collected by the alumni association and became the basis for the Heritage Protocol's collections. The second archivist made two statements that explain the development of the program. "In no uncertain terms, when the Heritage Protocol was established, it was an 'insurgent' project in direct competition with the University Archives." The emphasis on student-based materials came from a strong personal interest and not from the traditional role of a university archivist documenting the institutional record. "When we initiated the Heritage Protocol, we unwittingly emphasized this aspect of the university's history because I was not only the archivist but also an alumnus. As I have a natural fondness for my alma mater, I found documenting student life an appealing and attractive direction in which to take the program."[1] As a result this direction was supported by the founding group and continued until 2012.

The program created a central repository at the main campus library and decentralized "departmental archives" by using volunteer "ambassadors." These ambassadors were trained to document materials located in the areas under their purview and to create a collaborative online museum in the form of a website. The Heritage Protocol was run jointly by the university libraries, the alumni association, and University Relations with the archivist initially reporting to the library's associate dean for Access Services and later to the dean of the Libraries. A committee met regularly to develop programs and training. Later conversations focused on creating a physical museum to display the materials of the Heritage Protocol and to serve as a tool for institutional advancement.

Through generous donations from some of those same establishing individuals and a large effort by the associate director of University Relations and other staff, the Humanities Reading Room opened as the Heritage Museum in the fall of 2011. The bulk of the materials on display consisted of reproduced photographs from the existing collections and the state archives. The "permanent display" constituted a vivid time line of university history. Several movable cases with other display items, ceiling banners, stained glass windows with donor-funded glass medallions and shields, and ten large rectangular tables complemented the chronology in a formal, beautiful space in a building that is an excellent example of the Collegiate Gothic style of architecture prevalent on campuses in the 1920s.

After a personnel change in Special Collections and Archives in late 2012, the Heritage Protocol was moved into that division and was to be merged with University Archives. Although in many ways the Heritage Protocol created a comprehensive, collaborative, and campus-wide program, it suffered from some inherent challenges; decentralized archives are difficult to manage or provide access to without dedicated and skilled archival staff. A large managing committee, changes in personnel, and reliance on a single archivist created an environment that led to the decline of the program concept and its recognition on and off campus. As the committee stopped meeting, isolated collections of material remained all over campus only to be discovered years later.

From 2007 through 2013, the archivist and partners on campus, including the alumni association and University Relations, collected approximately one hundred linear feet of material. Although some previously mentioned elements of the program were successful only up to a point, the resulting set of materials gathered during this time made for an amazing collection that

illustrated the student experience at the university. The bulk of the items represented the 1920s through the 1960s, but items ranged from the 1850s to
the present. Some highlights included over one hundred scrapbooks, tens of
thousands of photographs, every yearbook, letterman sweaters, textiles, and
china dinnerware from various eras.

When I arrived at the university in December 2013, I came from a well-
established and organized university archive at another state institution. The
challenge of such an unusual program offered an opportunity to build on my
experience with institutional records and campus outreach. As an archivist I
found it exciting to work with content from a wider breadth of history (164
years). As the new archivist I needed time to understand and navigate the
unique circumstances of the Heritage Protocol initiative. The program's committee had not met for at least a year, the collections were stored in several
different locations and were in varying degrees of intellectual and physical
control, and the merger with University Archives had not yet taken place. My
first priorities included locating and identifying collections and organizing
the spaces, updating the collecting and campus-wide policy, preserving and
providing at least a basic description for everything identified, and engaging
current and new stakeholders.

SUDDEN AND UNEXPECTED
MANAGEMENT OF A QUASI MUSEUM

Six months into my position, the associate director of University Relations, who was heavily responsible for the development of the program and
museum, left the position and then the vice president for University Relations
agreed that the libraries should take full control of the space and contents.
For the past three years, the museum had been used for university-related
events and was occasionally open to the public. A small number of volunteers
from the departments that resided in other parts of the building oversaw the
museum. Maintaining access and an understanding of how to reach out to
potential students, alumni, community members, and others became a top
priority. The associate director for University Relations stated that "in addition to the museum, it will be used for very special events that will serve to
advance our university." My predecessor also indicated that from its beginnings and almost by accident, the museum was positioned as a public relations tool for the libraries, University Relations, and the alumni association.
Although nominally a museum, the exhibit functioned mostly as an institutional advancement space that was sometimes open to the public. Because
the exhibit lacked regular hours, exhibition schedules, or programming, it
would be difficult to call it a museum given current professional museum practice, though the intention was there during its initial creation. The museum

created a fund-raising initiative, which entailed selling stained glass windows of important groups or departments on campus to donors or campus entities. However, the development part of the program was in a holding pattern due to the changes taking place.

Coming from a background of teaching and working in museums, libraries, and archives, I immediately recognized that the particular story of this university's history was not as diverse and inclusive as it could be. Changes needed to occur if the institution hoped to engage and include the increasingly diverse student body. Although selections of what to display seemed innocent enough, they were made from and for the perspective of predominantly white southerners and for those who would be attracted to the nostalgia of the black-and-white 1940s–1960s photographs, which would also appeal to alumni donors of an earlier era. Documentary images of the first African American graduate and of the homecoming princess as well as significant African American student athletes are present, but other types of diversity are absent. For example, Latina and Asian women occasionally attended the women's college because they were considered "white" during the years following *Brown v. Board of Education* in 1954 and until and just after the Civil Rights Act of 1964, before full desegregation. In addition, religious and cultural diversity existed in clubs and in other types of student organizations. This diversity was documented in the yearbook, photograph, and scrapbook collections but not in the museum. Visiting students have made negative comments about how "white" and "male" the exhibit is, and African American faculty and staff have expressed their alienation from the university's history. It is likely that our other underrepresented and marginalized groups on campus have difficulty relating to the museum in a meaningful way.

It is important to consider the context of the creation of the exhibit and only fair to consider some of the challenges for the original organizers. They lacked early photographic materials to choose from. In addition, state-mandated racial segregation meant that African Americans and other marginalized groups were not part of the institution's history, and the bulk of materials initially accessioned had focused on some of the most exclusionary decades (1940s, 1950s, and early 1960s) of the university. Many exhibit images came from campus or yearbook photographers on assignment to portray certain aspects of campus life. Although present inclusion and diversity initiatives at the university have attempted to foster a more inclusive environment, the donation and collection of records and ephemera often take place decades after their creation and use, so the collection in the university archives has considerably less material available to document more of the current elements of diversity.

Personnel transitions complicated plans for the museum when the vice president of University Relations left just before the arrival of our new university president and was unable to finalize the plan with the library. With the two senior management positions left permanently vacant, the remaining office became resistant to continuing the transfer of authority for the space to the library and expressed concerns that the museum might be damaged by expanded access, such as regular student use or events deemed less appropriate than those hosted previously.

In this context, as policies and priorities took shape, parties understood the importance of the successful "Heritage" program brand. To honor the original program but to begin its transformation, we combined the names, and the outcome was the Heritage Protocol and University Archives (HPUA).

ENGAGING INTERNAL STAKEHOLDERS

A successful archives initiative requires that university colleagues recognize and understand the mission of institutional archives and explore ways to incorporate the value and importance of those archives into their daily work. Sometimes it was difficult for me to advocate for the archives with colleagues who spoke a different language. Even within the Special Collections and Archives Division, certain conversations have taken place about how the university archives functions and how its needs differ from those of the rest of the Special Collections and Archives Division. Colleagues need to be reminded of the importance of the archivist who is responsible for collecting institutional history under a campus-wide policy, building and maintaining relationships with every department, and articulating how the archives needs the ability to accession records through the institutional repository. The best way to accomplish engagement is through maintaining a strong presence, communicating frequently, and using resources strategically.

Communicating how archivists can provide assistance and collaborate with faculty, staff, and the community is essential. Examples of active participation include belonging to and participating in working groups and departments within libraries, such as the following.

> **Subject librarians:** These colleagues often work with faculty who are administrators of records or programs in their specific academic areas.
>
> **Digital Scholarship Working Group:** This group consists of staff as well as subject librarians, with the university archivist serving as an important resource. Although my work does not always translate directly into every digital scholarship activity, my readiness to jump in when needed keeps me visible and engaged with the other members of the group.
>
> **Learning Commons in the main campus library:** This department works with HPUA to staff the museum; department staff regularly hire and train students to work the service desks in the library.

Library administration: Support from library administrators is essential for acquiring funding and for fostering connections with those on and off campus whom archivists may not typically encounter.

Associate dean for Special Collections and Archives: This person plays an essential role in providing the budget and allocating resources to the program as well as offering strategic guidance. This department head also assists HPUA in understanding campus culture and politics.

EXTERNAL STAKEHOLDERS: ON CAMPUS

University employees outside the library frequently express a willingness to get involved because of the ways HPUA and the libraries support them and provide for their needs. Typically HPUA provides materials and information for everything, including web pages, events, publications, news releases, or various other projects. As HPUA establishes relationships with campus units, a natural second step involves assessing the historic records of academic and administrative departments and, it is hoped, transferring those records to the archive. Even with the campus-wide policy, there is always the need for some level of negotiation to create buy-in for all university departments, and in that way, they are similar to donors. These units may also share links to alumni of their colleges and programs. In some cases, patrons and alumni overlap and are both internal and external stakeholders depending on the context. For example, the university employs a number of alumni. Many of them work in administration and other vital staff positions, which greatly benefits the program, because they already appreciate the mission and aspirations of HPUA.

Here are examples of the main stakeholders on campus:

Library patrons: HPUA serves faculty, staff, students, and community members who want to access the collections and other information held within the program. Making these patrons aware of how to access HPUA collections is imperative for our mission, and their demand drives institutional efforts to expand collections and resources to provide access.

Records management: In earlier years, only limited communication occurred between the previous archivist and the University Records Management Liaison Officer (RMLO) located in Finance and Administration, likely due to the Heritage Protocol's ambiguous role of not being fully attached to the University Archives. After an initial meeting and after both parties became more familiar with each other's roles, the RMLO became a resource and assisted in helping ensure that office managers preserve anything with possible historic value for archival review before deeming the contents ready for destruction. The RMLO also facilitated the extremely smooth update of the Archival Materials Policy to the University Archives Policy that reflects the new version of HPUA and follows current archival best practices for college and university archives. This is an essential relationship because archives are part of the life cycle of records.

University Relations: As one of the previous comanagers of the campus program and current comanager of the museum space, this office still plays a role in the program. Currently facilities management and some scheduling for the museum remain shared responsibilities.

Alumni association: An original managing member of the program, the alumni association serves as a source of donations of physical collections and as our best connection for alumni outreach.

University Communications: This unit possesses the treasure trove of factual information and important contacts with external parties. HPUA possesses the raw material for future news and often provides historical items to go with press releases and articles.

General Counsel: Although some on campus feel intimidated by or are unfamiliar with the role of General Counsel, nothing is better than having a cadre of attorneys when help is needed.

University Development Foundation: This unit thrives on cultivating strong donor relations. Fortunately, the libraries have a development officer who frequently partners in developing events and other types of engagement with donors.

Student Government Association (SGA), clubs, and organizations: Partnering with student leaders seems like an obvious choice, especially due to the amount of student experience–based material being created as part of the institutional record.

Facilities: The program and the museum have several relationships with this department, including managing the spaces and coordinating the work of HPUA. Physical management of the spaces is sometimes more difficult because of the logistics and the mixture of who has authority over what.

Athletic department: At colleges and universities, athletic departments often manage their own archives, especially those related to the student athletes' personal information and statistics.

EXTERNAL STAKEHOLDERS—OFF CAMPUS

Off-campus stakeholders include entities and individuals who are essential for successful initiatives that directly contribute to the collections and to the funding of the program. Community patrons who use materials online and on-site are also valuable stakeholders.

> **Alumni:** Alumni donors through their ongoing engagement and support are a vital component of the program and one of the most enjoyable. The success of meetings and conversations with donors relies on HPUA's appreciating how alumni cherish their alma mater as well as being able to articulate how their involvement impacts the program.

> **News outlets:** Media outlets offer positive impact for HPUA while sharing content that benefits institutional research. A local television channel often visits campus and will stop by to do highlights for the evening news.

> **Community members and fans:** Those who are extended members of the university community may be family and friends of alumni or people who are simply fans and have collected material over the years. Community organizations also offer partnership and outreach opportunities.

EVOLUTION AND EXPANSION OF THE PROGRAM

HPUA strives to be a streamlined university archives with a decidedly "heritage" flavor that attracts all campus partners for what it can contribute to events and experiences as well as for its role as an accessible repository for primary sources. History is a way to connect to an institution. New and former students share in the collective past of the institution, and good archival programs can foster a sense of dedication, loyalty, and connection to something greater and long-standing. With all these stakeholders engaged on some level, considerable effort will be invested in maintaining these relationships as the program develops. Outreach, engagement, and advocacy build on the progress made in the past and will propel the program toward these goals:

> **Website and social media:** The Facebook page for the program had about eight hundred "likes" in December 2013. After strategically planning what is posted and when, as well as creating a direct relationship with the university's Facebook page, the HPUA page has gotten three times more traffic and had 1,840 "likes" in August 2016.

Public and private events: HPUA regularly provides tours and talks and has an interactive table at on- and off-campus events.

Exhibits: Each year, an exhibit lasting several months adorns the Special Collections and Archives Gallery in the main campus library.

The Heritage Reading Room: Located in the main campus library, the reading room occupies a space adjacent to the office and workroom for HPUA. It is a well-appointed, quiet study and exhibit space that is often used for small, private events or meetings. The exhibit cases allow for highlighting collections of HPUA's choosing or creating exhibits that can coincide with new acquisitions or other campus events.

The Heritage Museum: Though the space is called a museum, currently it is an event space with a "permanent" photographic (reproductions) exhibit in the cases lining the walls to create a visual time line. To create an effective museum and an outreach tool as well as a space for students and the community to use, we will focus on making the museum a public space that engages patrons with Florida State University's history in a dynamic way.

Heritage Museum executive and advisory boards: In 2015, in order to move forward with work on the museum and in turn create direct positive impact on the overall program, the associate dean for Special Collections and Archives sought to revive the original Heritage Protocol committee. The plan was to bring back several people and groups from on and off campus who were previously committed to the museum and programs, especially fund-raising.

ASSESSMENT

In all programs, keeping track of accomplishments not only helps illustrate where resources are successfully spent but also helps determine whether those choices are useful in future planning. Statistics and tangible evidence are necessary to make the case for additional resources; proving need can be a motivating factor for receiving those resources from administrative and donor sources. Even small successes show the potential for larger ones and should be so noted. In the case of HPUA, this success is apparent in the documented increase in museum attendance, reference requests, and the number of tours and events. Also useful is tracking the amount of materials acquired, collected, and processed as well as the number of reproduction requests. Though never asked to do so, I have created an annual report for HPUA for the past two years that has been a useful internal reference to have on hand for creating presentations and for donor meetings.

CONCLUSION: LEARNING TO MAKE IT ALL WORK

What happens when the university archives are entwined with a separate, previously created program with several stakeholders?

Understanding the playing field and the players is essential and takes time. Hitting the ground running is also essential because there is much work to do. Therefore, decisions that seem obvious need time to develop and require some research into the past. That awareness comes through working with individuals previously associated with the programs, reaching out to colleagues outside the institution to compare perspectives, and reviewing past documentation. In the case of HPUA, it involved determining the existing parts of the program, what they consisted of (collections, patrons, facilities), and how they fit into the landscape (stakeholders, funding, current understanding of the function of the program) and then determining the expectations and possibilities and making a plan.

During the evolution and expansion of such a multifaceted initiative, how do staff and stakeholders find the way to the other side?

Proper planning prevents poor performance in most cases, so having a strategic plan that will be flexible as things change is very important. However, even with the best preparation, there will be decisions that have unknowable consequences. and that result has to be acceptable or nothing will ever be completed. It's about doing due diligence and then making confident decisions. It is learning to balance, pivot, and adjust, accepting failures, celebrating successes, and always moving forward.

Keeping internal and external stakeholders involved along the way honors past contributions and keeps them invested in the program. For immediate staff, it is important to give context to decisions and assignments so that staff members feel they are moving toward a goal versus picking away at a never-ending list of seemingly unrelated or low-impact projects. That does not mean explaining and justifying every decision, but it does mean including the staff in the larger idea as it evolves. Complex, long-term projects require dedication, and there is nothing worse than staff who are feeling that their work is not moving anything in the right direction or that they have no input in the process.

In terms of advocacy, you must have a "go-to" spiel about your program that you can spin for whatever situation you are in. Colleges and universities are small towns; you will run into everyone you know, and everyone knows someone whom you know and they may be able to further your cause. This proximity has created numerous opportunities for our program.

In serving as the program archivist, the challenge of learning what to do and when to do it was common. The most difficult task was leading with a small staff and regularly multitasking to balance too many things. For all the potential and expectations of the program and museum, there remains significant need for additional full-time staff. With administrative and donor support, the development plans, and new boards, I believe some of the overload may be alleviated in the coming year.

I learned that though perfection can remain an aspirational goal, it rarely, if ever, is achieved, so having to settle for what can be accomplished given the circumstances took a change of attitude and perspective as well as a new level of patience. Reprioritizing of tasks, schedules, and preferences is a must, and sometimes things that are important must wait. Reaching out to others in the library and on campus who can be of assistance has been useful in untangling some of the more complicated issues.

Engaging internal and external stakeholders takes considerable activity in many different arenas. Not all attempts at engagement will be successful. As an archivist, keeping extensive notes for each component of the program allows for documenting both best practices and lessons learned. Sometimes one has to sunset a particular project or revisit a group that has records of interest at a more convenient time. Balancing the program with patron needs and leveraging resources against expenditures and outcomes are much easier to do when one knows the landscape of the program, the library, and the campus community. The many stakeholders associated with this initiative all play important roles. All this coordination, effort, and stress allows the HPUA to fulfill its mission to acquire, preserve, and provide access to the history of the university and its predecessor institutions. Without the engagement of current students, faculty, staff, and community members, this initiative cannot continue building these collections that represent the past of the institution and its community.

NOTE

1. Eddie Woodward, "Heritage Protocol at Florida State University," *Journal of Archival Organization* 11, no. 1–2 (2013): 83–112, doi:10.1080/15332748 .2013.884402.

CHRISTINA L. WISSINGER, PhD

14

The Closing of a Library

Using Gilbert's Behavior Engineering Model to Manage Innovative Change

THE J. S. L. LIBRARY'S ADMINISTRATION planned to close the physical library building. This plan required the conversion of resources from print to electronic as well as the restructuring of library departments and retraining of library employees. The library administration's plan was to replace print materials with electronic resources in an attempt to move to a completely virtual library and embed library services into academic departments across the university. The plan to close the library was controversial, on campus and within the library community. Because this conversion had never been attempted at the university, library employees faced challenges, problems, and resistance in their transition to a new service model. This case study will summarize the transitions that library liaisons and other library staff faced during this change. In addition, this case study will illustrate how Gilbert's behavior engineering model (BEM) could have been used as a framework for reinvention and how other libraries may use BEM as a guide for implementing and managing change. Whether you applaud or oppose the library administration's plan, it is important to analyze this case. As libraries of various types (public, private, and academic) are increasingly being asked to prove their value and learn to stretch their budgets, the need for innovative yet untested service models may become a reality for many libraries in the next decade.

BACKGROUND

The J. S. L Library is a well-established, private academic library founded in the 1920s and supporting mostly graduate students, teaching faculty, and researchers. The J. S. L. Library can be considered a branch library; however, its size makes it equal to general libraries at many academic institutions. The library provides resources and services to a user group of more than twelve thousand students, staff, and faculty. The library's main user areas are the health and biological sciences. As the availability of online resources increased, the necessity of having a physical library came into question. Because the J. S. L. Library focuses on the life sciences, the library had the advantage of a large and growing number of online resources. This depth and breadth of online resources supporting the library's user areas gave library administrators the ability to legitimately consider moving to a fully virtual collection with library services solely embedded in academic departments. In addition, the daily data collected by the library supported the move to close the physical library building. The average number of people who walked through the doors of the library to check out physical items dramatically decreased with the proliferation of e-journals and e-books. For example, the number of users who entered the library on a typical day was approximately one hundred and of those people, fewer than half checked out books; however, on the same day tens of thousands of e-articles were downloaded from the collection. One effect of decreasing on-site use and increasing online use was a reduction in the number of library employees who were necessary for maintaining a print collection. At one time the J. S. L. Library employed around ninety individuals; however, at the time of the transition, the employees of the library totaled roughly fifty individuals. Consequently, as the number of employees was reduced, part of the personnel budget was reallocated to the expanding electronic collection.

These changes led the library's administration to adopt a dramatically different service model. The change was systemic: public services departments changed the physical locations where they provided services, acquisitions placed a priority on the growth of electronic resources and reduced print purchases to only essential items not available electronically, and emphasis was placed on enhancing the library's virtual presence because all interaction with resources would take place through the library's website. The traditional library service model of having users come into the physical library to use resources and services needed to be restructured to allow library users to stay in their department offices or labs and have resources and services come to them.

The library liaison program was revamped with the goal of fully embedding subject librarians in the academic departments they serve as opposed to liaisons having offices in the library. The embedded service model required liaison librarians to do the majority of their work outside the library building to enhance the integration of library services into the daily work of the departments they served. The library liaison program refocused on hiring new librarians with specific subject expertise. Library department heads were the only liaisons who were not new hires; however, they were assigned liaison activities and were expected to embed into academic departments where possible. In combination with the restructuring of the library liaison program, library staff responsible for managing the print collection in circulation, binding, reserves, and other on-site services were asked to provide detailed descriptions of their job duties.

Although the core duties of library liaisons remained similar to those of traditional reference librarians at academic institutions, library staff were required to significantly change their skills. Staff were asked to catalog the skills needed to do their jobs and list new job skills they would be interested in learning. This information allowed library administration to attempt to place staff in new roles aligning previous skills and current interests. The goal was to make the transition for library staff as comfortable as possible. However, some staff were concerned that the cataloging of their skills would be used to lay off staff. Library administration was adamantly opposed to layoffs; however, despite the administration's statement against layoffs, staff concerns persisted.

GILBERT'S BEHAVIOR ENGINEERING MODEL

Thomas F. Gilbert has been called the "father of performance improvement." He was an innovator in the field of behavioral analysis, coined the term "performance engineering," and was the first Honorary Life Member of the International Society for Performance Improvement.[1] Gilbert's book *Human Competence: Engineering Worthy Performance*, first published in 1978 and reprinted in 2007, is critically acclaimed and regularly used as a text in the fields of business, instructional systems, instructional design, and educational technology. Gilbert's Behavior Engineering Model (BEM), updated by Roger Chevalier, is used to place a structure on the case of the J. S. L. Library (table 14.1). BEM separates what an employee brings to the job, or an individual's "repertory of behavior," from environmental elements that "encourage or impede performance."[2] BEM is a useful model to guide organizations attempting to institute change. Because BEM focuses on factors that employees face when undergoing changes to their jobs, it can be used as a framework to successfully transition employees' roles. BEM is also a diagnostic tool for finding potential performance problems. It is important to note that BEM is not a set

TABLE 14.1

Updated Behavior Engineering Model

	Information	Resources	Incentives
ENVIRONMENT	• Roles and performance expectations are clearly defined; employees are given relevant and frequent feedback about the adequacy of performance. • Clear and relevant guides are used to describe the work process. • The performance management system guides employee performance and development.	• Materials, tools, and time needed to do the job are present. • Processes and procedures are clearly defined and enhance individual performance if followed. • Overall physical and psychological work environment contributes to improved performance; work conditions are safe, clear, organized, and conducive to performance.	• Financial and nonfinancial incentives are present; measurement and reward systems reinforce positive performance. • Jobs are enriched to allow for fulfillment of employee needs. • Overall work environment is positive, where employees believe they have an opportunity to succeed; career development opportunities are present.
	Knowledge/Skills	**Capacity**	**Motives**
INDIVIDUAL	• Employees have the necessary knowledge, experience, and skills to do the desired behaviors. • Employees with the necessary knowledge, experience, and skills are properly placed to use and share what they know. • Employees are cross-trained to understand each other's roles.	• Employees have the capacity to learn and do what is needed to perform successfully. • Employees are recruited and selected to match the realities of the work situation. • Employees are free of emotional limitations that would interfere with their performance.	• Motives of employees are aligned with the work and the work environment. • Employees desire to perform the required jobs. • Employees are recruited and selected to match the realities of the work situation.

SOURCE: Roger Chevalier, "Updating the Behavior Engineering Model," *Performance Improvement* 42, no. 5 (2003): 8–14.

of best practices but a model for guiding change. BEM is useful for organizations attempting the untested, providing a structure for identifying potential problems when creating an unknown service model or attempting a change in organizational structure or work environment.

As the library faced the restructuring of its service model and attempted to reenvision its positions, the administration worked without a model. In retrospect BEM would have been an ideal model for library administration to use during the transition and would have given library administration a framework to guide decisions. The following section will illustrate how BEM aligns with the library's most successful restructuring, the library liaisons, and how it could have facilitated the transition for staff, reducing stress and anxiety.

BEM: AN AMBIDEXTROUS MODEL

Traditionally, BEM is a systematic troubleshooting process in which the factors are considered in a specific order (see table 14.1). One starts with the three categories under *Environment* moving from left to right (*Information, Resources, Incentives*). Afterward, the three categories under *Individual* are reviewed moving from right to left (*Motives, Capacity, Knowledge/Skills*). For this case study, BEM would have been best employed moving in the traditional direction just stated for the library liaisons and moving in the reverse direction for library staff. Although BEM was designed to move in the traditional order, for the library staff I will show how using BEM in reverse would have been more effective. This case is unique in that it presents the use of BEM for guiding an untested service model, and it suggests that BEM can be used successfully in the traditional order and in reverse order, depending on the climate of the organization undergoing transition.

BEM APPLIED TO CHANGES IN THE LIBRARY LIAISON ROLE

Library liaisons function the same way as subject librarians at many other academic research libraries. The liaison's goal is to become embedded in an assigned academic department. In addition to responding to reference questions and guiding collection development, the liaisons must embed themselves physically in the units they serve and become integrated into the research culture of their liaison departments. Library liaisons use embedding to facilitate research projects and create collaborative working relationships with researchers and students. Because this type of work depends on the ubiquity of electronic resources and locations near faculty offices, liaisons faced significant changes to their job but had the most job security and support from library administration during the transition.

To illustrate how the library liaison program aligns with the BEM model, we begin with *Environment* factors, focusing first on *Information*. The goals of the reenvisioned liaison program were clearly laid out internally within the organization's structure and externally through marketing efforts on the library's website. *Resources* were reallocated from print to online, and laptops and other mobile technologies were provided for the library liaisons to work with their assigned departments located outside the library. *Incentives* were built into the transition as well. Liaisons doing exceptional work, such as setting up office hours in an academic department or contributing to a collaborative research project within an academic department, were publicly recognized. In addition, library administration provided a special salary award to recognize staff members who excelled in their work.

The other area of BEM focuses on the *Individual* beginning with *Motives*. The criteria for *Motives* were apparent in the liaison job description. Job advertisements were clearly written to emphasize advanced subject degrees. In addition, job descriptions specified the embedded aspect of the job as well as the desire for collaboration and working within assigned departments located outside the library. *Capacity* was addressed in job descriptions and recruitment efforts through an emphasis on library experience, advanced subject degrees, and the ability to independently promote the library's new service model. The third and final *Individual* focus is on *Knowledge/Skills*. In addition to training opportunities provided by professional associations, liaison librarians had the opportunity to meet with librarians from a local university to discuss the differences and similarities between their respective services models. Also, liaisons had professional development funds to attend conferences that would assist them in successfully embedding into their assigned academic departments.

The library liaison program was highly successful according to several scholarly articles and professional presentations that showcased the program. Currently, the library employs eleven liaisons; there were six liaisons during the transition period. Although the library administration was not aware of BEM at the time of the innovation, the close alignment of the library's liaison program with BEM illustrates how BEM can be used to facilitate the transition to an innovative new service model for professional librarians.

BEM APPLIED TO LIBRARY STAFF CHANGES

The planned closing of the library's physical building required library staff to find alternative job duties. Library departments affected by the changes included monographs cataloging, circulation, information desk services, and reserves. Typically, staff were responsible for loaning and collecting circulating materials, sorting and re-shelving materials, cataloging and repairing materials, issuing library cards, and performing other clerical tasks. When a physical library location is closed, these traditional job duties become unnecessary due to the removal of on-site materials.

Library administration planned to retrain current staff to avoid any layoffs. Although administration saw retraining as a viable option, staff requiring retraining were apprehensive and unsure of their current role in the evolving library structure. The anxiety, related to the unknown future of their jobs, led to low morale and tension. Library administration was aware of the low morale and anxiety in library staff; however, there was no plan in place to resolve the problem.

For library staff, using BEM in its traditional order was not likely to help them cope with the transitions they needed to make. The majority of library staff had been with the organization for over a decade and held the positions undergoing the most significant changes. These staff members were emotionally invested in the library and would benefit from BEM when applied in the reverse direction beginning with emotional factors. In some situations, the job duties that had been done for decades would no longer exist, and the staff would be asked to learn a completely new set of job skills. In addition, the staff felt left out of the decision to close the physical library because they were not consulted. They also felt that they were not consulted when discussions took place regarding how their jobs would change. To support the transitions required by staff, BEM should be used in the reverse direction, beginning with the *Individual* factors and focusing first on *Motives,* then on *Capacity* and then on *Knowledge/Skills. Environment* factors should follow, beginning with *Information,* then *Resources,* and finally *Incentives.*

The emotional areas of BEM need to be addressed first to calm fears and anxieties and place staff in an open mind-set to collaborate on the restructuring. Applying BEM in the traditional direction, as suggested for the library liaisons who were mostly new hires, would not successfully guide the changes staff were being asked to make. *Individual* factors should be addressed starting with *Motives.* Library staff need to feel motivated to make significant changes to their jobs. Their voices need to be heard and valued when their positions are being redesigned. The library liaisons were consulted regularly and included in strategic discussions, so motivation was not a problem that they faced during the transition. Because library staff faced the greatest potential to be laid off in the new service model, job security must be addressed and falls within the area of *Motives.* As part of *Capacity,* staff should be asked to share their areas of interest and areas they would not feel comfortable working in. The *Knowledge/Skills* section of BEM should ensure that employees are given multiple training opportunities and are provided with the resources necessary to adapt to a new type of work. No employee should be reassigned to a new area without training, support, and mentoring.

Moving on to *Environment* factors, *Information* should be addressed first. Each staff member needs a clear description of the new job as well as a clear understanding of how success or failure in the new position will be assessed. The *Resources* component can determine whether software or hardware is required for the new position, how these resources will be obtained, and how training will be provided. Finally, *Incentives* need to be in place focusing on successful transitions into new job duties and positions. This component should include the library administration's recognition and highlighting of successful staff transitions using internal communication channels and employee events. Acknowledgments of success should be clear and immediate, and library staff should be rewarded for their efforts to adapt to new service models.

BEM AREAS NOT APPLIED TO STAFF TRANSITIONS

During the closing of the library, the administration covered some of the areas in BEM related to staff changes without being aware of the model; however, several areas were not covered. *Capacity* and *Knowledge/Skills* were addressed when staff were asked to share their interests in new job opportunities and were assured that they would be provided with the time and training necessary for changing job duties. Also, although *Resources* and *Incentives* were not covered, this omission would have little effect on the transition because these components are implemented after the change of job duties has occurred.

The most significant issues related to staff changes were the areas in BEM that were not addressed. The decision to close the library building was a top-down decision. Comments and concerns from library staff occurred after the decision had been made and announced. For the *Motives* section of BEM to be successfully implemented, the staff needed to be aware of, and involved in, critical decision-making meetings early in the process, which would facilitate buy-in and mitigate resistance and negativity associated with the new service model. In addition, *Information* was not addressed. New job descriptions were not available for staff at the time they were made aware of the library closing or when they were asked to catalog their job skills. Because staff did not have documentation illustrating what new jobs would require, it was difficult for them to understand what their role would be in the new service model. This lack of transparency resulted in apprehension and increased anxieties among the staff. If the BEM model had been employed in reverse order, the changes staff were being asked to make may have been accepted more easily and with less stress and trepidation.

QUESTIONS TO ASK WHEN USING BEM

BEM may be used in the traditional direction typically found in the scholarly literature or in the reverse direction suggested in this case depending on the type of jobs requiring changes and the type of employees who are being asked to change (newly hired employees or long-time ones). If an organization is attempting to make a significant change, the first questions to ask are these:

Which jobs will require the greatest changes to skill sets? and Which type of employees hold these positions? For long-term employees who have demonstrated commitment to the job, BEM may be more effectively employed in the reverse direction. Addressing *Motives* and *Capacity* first may provide staff with a better understanding of what changes may occur and how staff fit into the new model. Asking individuals to make significant changes to jobs they have occupied for decades requires library administration to consider employee's emotional factors. Using BEM in reverse gives employees time and support to adjust psychologically to the transitions before being asked to categorize their job duties and learn new skills in unknown areas of the library. When an organization is creating something new that requires the significant restricting of a program and hiring of new employees, BEM can be used in the traditional order as shown in the liaison program, which was highly successful and aligned closely with the traditional progression through BEM.

WHAT WE CAN LEARN FROM J. S. L. LIBRARY

Ultimately, the proposal to close the physical library was abandoned. However, the library hired several new liaisons, and all the library liaisons were moved out of the library building. The liaisons obtained offices outside the library, either in a building that previously housed another department of the library or at several locations across the campus where they have office hours in their assigned departments.

The library building is open from 9 a.m. to 6 p.m. Monday through Friday and from 10 a.m. to 4 p.m. on Saturdays; the building is closed on Sundays. The building maintains a small number of library staff focused on circulating the remaining print collection, providing document delivery services, and assisting with basic reference questions. Staff not related to the circulation of materials or on-site user needs moved off-site to a location approximately twenty minutes by university shuttle from the main campus.

Although the library administration did not achieve its initial goal of closing the building, the attempt to create an innovative library model can teach us several things. The most compelling factor is that significant change can more easily occur when new employees are hired into positions that exemplify a new way of doing the work. The alignment of the BEM model with the library liaison program illustrates how BEM can facilitate innovation. Although the library administration did not use BEM when creating and implementing the new service model, the success of the liaison program supports the use of BEM for future change because it illustrates the way this case and BEM align. When long-term staff are asked to make significant changes and adopt a new service model, the transitions are more difficult to implement. The case of J. S. L. Library shows how BEM can be used in the reverse direction to facilitate change for long-term employees who are being asked to significantly change their job duties. Change is a difficult process, especially when the change is new and has not been implemented before at the institution. Using BEM as a framework may allow organizations to avoid potentially stressful situations for employees and provide support to libraries attempting innovative and untested change. Although other models for engineering human performance are available in the scholarly literature, this case illustrates the flexibility of BEM to support changes in two different types of employee groups.

NOTES

1. Thomas F. Gilbert, *Human Competence: Engineering Worthy Performance* (New York: John Wiley and Sons, 2007).
2. Roger Chevalier, "Updating the Behavior Engineering Model," *Performance Improvement* 42, no. 5 (2003): 8–14.

About the Editors and Contributors

EDITORS

TAMMY NICKELSON DEARIE currently serves as interim university librarian at the University of California, San Diego where she is responsible for the library-wide services of business and finance, capital planning, facilities, human resources, information technology services, internal communications, and safety and security. The library's Diversity and Inclusion Committee, Community Building Committee, and Environmental Sustainability Committee are part of her portfolio. She has served on numerous committees at the national level and system-wide within the University of California. She is a member of the editorial boards for the *Journal of Access Services* and the *Journal of Interlibrary Loan, Document Delivery and Electronic Reserve.* Ms. Dearie earned her master of library and information science degree from the University of California, Los Angeles and her bachelor of arts in history with a minor in women's studies from the University of California, San Diego.

MICHAEL METH is the associate dean, Research and Learning Services at the Florida State University (FSU) Libraries. Michael's portfolio includes responsibility for the Learning Commons (undergraduate services), Scholars Commons (graduate and faculty services), and STEM Libraries as well as the Assessment and Engagement units of the University Libraries. Prior to his current role at FSU, Michael was the director of the Ontario Institute for Studies in Education (OISE) Library at the University of Toronto (UofT). Michael has taught at UofT's iSchool and in the Department of Management at UofT Mississauga. Prior to this appointment at OISE, Michael was the director of the Li Koon Chun Finance Learning Centre at the UofT Mississauga Library. He has a master of information studies degree from the Faculty of Information Studies (UofT) and a bachelor of business administration degree from the Schulich School of Business (York University). Michael is an active member of the library and university communities, having served in leadership roles with the UofT iSchool Alumni Association and the Special Libraries Association (SLA). In 2014, Michael was selected as a Senior Fellow at UCLA's Graduate School of Education and Information Studies, and in 2013 he participated in Harvard's Leadership Institute for Academic Librarians.

ELAINE L. WESTBROOKS is vice provost for university libraries and university librarian, University of North Carolina at Chapel Hill. She provides support for the research enterprise's short- and long-term objectives as well as operational leadership to subject specialists who represent the arts and humanities, social sciences, international studies, and science and engineering. Elaine's previous positions include associate dean of Libraries at the University of Nebraska–Lincoln and head of Metadata Services at Cornell University. She is the coeditor of *Metadata in Practice* (2004). She has presented her research at various conferences, including the American Library Association, the Coalition for Networked Information, Dublin Core, and the Library and Information Technology Association. Because of her efforts to build strategic partnerships across borders, Elaine was the recipient of the Foreign Expert Award from Fudan University in Shanghai, China, in 2015. In 2005 she received the Chancellor's Award for Excellence in Librarianship from the State University of New York. In 2014 Elaine was a Senior Fellow at UCLA's Graduate School of Education and Information Studies. She has a BA in linguistics and an MLIS from the University of Pittsburgh.

CONTRIBUTORS

M. H. ALBRO is the STEM librarian at Shippensburg University in south-central Pennsylvania. Her research interests are data management and assessment and library involvement in student research. She has been involved with strategic planning steering at the libraries of Clemson University and Shippensburg University.

MAURITA BALDOCK was the assistant librarian and archivist at the University of Arizona's Special Collections from 2013 until 2016. Previous to her time there, she worked at the library at the New-York Historical Society for thirteen years. She is currently the supervisory archivist in the Preparation Section of the Manuscript Division at the Library of Congress. She received her master's degree in history and a certificate in archival management from New York University and her master's degree in library and information science from the Pratt Institute.

H. AUSTIN BOOTH is the vice provost for University Libraries at the University at Buffalo. In this position, she oversees the largest library system within the State University of New York (SUNY) system, including the Law Library and the Health Sciences Library. She holds an MA in English from the University of Michigan and an MLIS from the University of California, Berkeley as well as a BA in English and a BA in economics from Cornell University. Ms. Booth's publications include two coedited books from MIT Press on gender and cyberculture as well as journal articles and book chapters on evidence-based health care, instructional design, and cultural studies.

SIAN BRANNON, associate dean for Collection Management at University of North Texas Libraries, has been in libraries since the 1990s. She has worked in public, academic, and technical libraries, but likes her home library the best. Her research interests include supervision and leadership, internships, assessment, fear of negative evaluation, and, randomly, the Technology Acceptance Model. She edits *Public Services Quarterly* and is an adjunct professor for technical services courses. When not library-ing, she, well, doesn't do much else because she is always library-ing.

YOLANDA COOPER is the university librarian at Emory University in Atlanta, Georgia. Prior to her move to Emory, she held two positions at the University of Miami, in Miami, Florida, from 2006 to 2013, first as the deputy university librarian and then as acting dean and university librarian. She is the author of a chapter in *Identity Palimpsests* that focuses on the development of a collaborative archive from the African diaspora in south Florida and has spoken most recently on collaborative efforts with Georgia Institute of Technology and other surrounding institutions in Georgia.

KATHRYN M. CROWE is associate dean for Public Services at the University Libraries at the University of North Carolina at Greensboro. She has overall responsibility for the Libraries' services, assessment, and marketing and outreach. Kathryn publishes and presents internationally, nationally, and regionally on library assessment, leadership, and public services.

MICHAEL A. CRUMPTON, MLS, SPHR, is the assistant dean for Administrative Services at the University of North Carolina at Greensboro. Mike oversees administration of budgets, human resources, and facilities and organizes and addresses space and remodeling issues. He is an adjunct instructor for the Department of Library and Information Studies at the University of North Carolina at Greensboro and is certified as a Senior Human Resources Professional. His published works include *Handbook for Community College Librarians* (Libraries Unlimited, 2013), *Strategic Human Resource Planning for Academic Libraries* (Chandos Publishing, 2015), and chapters and articles in his institutional repository at http://libres.uncg.edu/ir/uncg/clist.aspx?id=1946.

KATHLEEN DELONG is an associate university librarian (AUL) with the University of Alberta Libraries. As well as her MLIS and master's in public management from the University of Alberta, she completed a doctorate at Simmons College. As a member of the 8Rs research team, she has been involved in two major studies: "The Future of Human Resources in Canadian Libraries" examined human resources issues across Canada, and "8Rs Redux" investigated current issues in Canadian research libraries. Most recently, Kathleen has taught the Leadership and Management course for the library school at the University of Alberta. To sum up, Kathleen continues to be inspired by practice, research, and teaching.

LISA HANSON O'HARA is the acting associate university librarian, Research Support Services at the University of Manitoba Libraries. Lisa has published on topics as varied as Google Scholar, collection use, and implementing and testing discovery layers in libraries and has spoken numerous times on the changing work in library technical services.

SCOTT HOLLANDER has served as an electronic resources librarian, web manager, and interim coordinator of Digital Collections since arriving at the University at Buffalo Libraries in 1995. In his current position, Scott maintains accountability for the overall direction, design, acquisition, installation, and secure operation of all technology used by the University at Buffalo Libraries. He also directs the development and coordination of the Libraries' platforms supporting digital scholarship. In 2014, Scott won the SUNY Chancellor's Award for Excellence in Professional Service. Scott holds a bachelor's degree in economics, with a minor in computer science, from Canisius College and an MLS degree from the University at Buffalo.

AMY HARRIS HOUK is the head of the Research, Outreach, and Instruction Department at the University of North Carolina at Greensboro (UNCG). In this role she oversees the liaison program. She also served as a member of the task force that recommended the library's current liaison structure. Previously she was information literacy coordinator at UNCG. Her primary research interests are pedagogy and assessment.

SARAH KEEN is the university archivist, the head of Special Collections and University Archives, and an associate professor in the Colgate University Libraries. Previously she worked at the Division of Rare and Manuscript Collections at Cornell University and at the Sophia Smith Collection at Smith College. Sarah is an alumna of the 2015 Archives Leadership Institute and is a member of the Society of American Archivists, the Mid-Atlantic Regional Archives Conference, and ARMA International. She earned her BA from Alma College and her MSI with a specialization in archives and records management from the University of Michigan's School of Information.

BRIAN WILLIAM KEITH is the associate dean for Administrative Services and Faculty Affairs at the George A. Smathers Libraries, University of Florida. He is the most senior facilities and security, human resources, staff development, financial, and grants management professional for the Smathers Libraries. Keith has a distinguished history of service to the profession at the national level and to the university and has noteworthy accomplishments in research and scholarship, including serving as a principal investigator. He is also a recipient of the SirsiDynix-ALA-APA Award for Outstanding Achievement in Promoting Salaries and Status for Library Workers.

CHARLES LYONS is the associate university librarian for Discovery and Delivery in the UB Libraries at the University at Buffalo (SUNY). He began his career in the UB Libraries as the subject librarian for business and management and after attaining tenure he served as the electronic resources librarian. Before coming to UB, Charles worked in the corporate library at Lehman Brothers in New York City and in the Science and Engineering Libraries at the University of Virginia.

LES MOOR is head of Technical Services at the University of Manitoba Libraries. Before his current appointment he was assistant manager of the OCLC contract cataloging office in Winnipeg, Manitoba, Canada. Les is interested in library acquisitions, collections, and cataloging and metadata and in developing applications to support some of these activities.

CATHERINE MURRAY-RUST is currently the vice provost for Learning Excellence and dean of Libraries at the Georgia Institute of Technology. She has administrative responsibility for several academic programs, 160 faculty and staff, almost 500,000 square feet of central campus space, and a library budget of about $14 million. She previously served as the dean of Libraries at Colorado State University and associate university librarian at Oregon State University. She worked at Cornell University Libraries for more than twenty years in a variety of positions, including reference librarian, training and implementation librarian in the Systems Office, and associate university librarian.

VERÓNICA REYES-ESCUDERO is borderlands curator for Special Collections at the University of Arizona Libraries. She works with faculty and students across disciplines in using special collections materials and engages the community through events that highlight the archives' rich holdings on the U.S.–Mexico borderlands. Verónica was previously a subject specialist for English literature, French, and Italian. She has written and presented on incorporating archives-based research into the curriculum, the intersection of special collections and the digital humanities, and the archives of Mexican American literary authors. She recently coauthored *Latinos in Libraries, Museums, and Archives: Cultural Competence in Action! An Asset-Based Approach*.

MEGAN SHEFFIELD is the e-science librarian at Clemson University. Her research has focused on data management and on academic library service models. She has written articles and presented at conferences on creating new library services, making "single service point" transitions, and guiding librarians through times of change.

LAURA I. SPEARS, PhD, is the associate assessment librarian with the University of Florida, George A. Smathers Libraries. Her recent dissertation, awarded by Florida State University, examined library value as expressed in social media used for public library funding advocacy. Her publications include several studies of technology deployment in diverse communities, including studies of children, broadband access, and broadband measurement in public libraries, and multiple publications on IT education with the Florida State University Information Institute.

CECILIA TELLIS lives and breathes academic librarianship and cannot recall a time when she wasn't thinking of creative and innovative ways to improve a user's library experience. In 2004 she began her career at McGill University's Nahum Gelber Law Library and then moved on to the Brian Dickson

Law Library at the University of Ottawa, where she extensively taught legal research. Since 2009 she has been at the Management Library at the University of Ottawa, where she provides bilingual (English–French), client-oriented, and enthusiastic service. She believes anyone can learn to lead and sincerely hopes that new information professionals explore and create leadership opportunities throughout their careers.

SANDRA VARRY is the Heritage Protocol and university archivist at Florida State University (FSU) where she collects for, manages, and provides access to FSU's archives and manages its Heritage Museum. She holds an MFA in photography from the University of North Carolina at Chapel Hill and an MLIS from the University of South Florida. She became a certified archivist in 2013 and a digital archives specialist in 2014. She is Immediate Past President of the Society of Florida Archivists and is currently the Society of American Archivists' Key Contact for Florida. She taught traditional and digital photography for thirteen years before becoming a full-time archivist, specializing in historic photograph collections.

CHRISTINA L. WISSINGER, PhD, is a tenure track faculty member with The Pennsylvania State University Libraries. In addition to her PhD, she holds a master's degree in library and information science from the University of Pittsburgh. Her research has been presented at the American Anthropological Association Conference, National Communications Ethics Conference, and Pennsylvania Library Association Conference. Dr. Wissinger has published in the *Journal of Social Media Studies, Proceedings of Society for Information Technology and Teacher Education,* and the American Foundation for the Blind's trade publication *Access World.* Her research interests focus on the areas of literacy, privacy, and informed consent.

INDEX